IRELAND

The Union and its aftermath

OLIVER MACDONAGH

London
GEORGE ALLEN & UNWIN LTD.
Ruskin House   Museum Street

This revised and enlarged edition first published in 1977

ISBN 0 04 941004 0 hardback
ISBN 0 04 941005 9 paperback

The first edition of this book was published in the USA by Prentice Hall, Inc. in 1968

Printed in Great Britain
in 10 on 11 point Times New Roman
by Clarke, Doble & Brendon Ltd,
Plymouth

To my daughters, Clodagh, Mary,
Emer and Melisa

Contents

Preface

The preface to the original book, of which the present work is a revision and extension, was written in 1967, and began:

> The present author regards the Act of Union as the most important single factor in shaping Ireland as a nation in the modern world. Of course, the condition of subordination to Great Britain deeply influenced almost every Irish development for several centuries before 1800. But this subordination took on a radically different form under the Act of Union, the effects of which governed Irish politics and even many aspects of Irish social and economic life long after the achievement of independence. The experience of being assimilated by, and resisting assimilation into, a powerful and alien empire – perhaps the master-culture of the nineteenth century – was truly traumatic. It is only within the last decade that the sufferer has shown certainly that he is recovering from the successive shocks of fusion and severance.

In 1975 it seems all too clear that the announcement of recovery was premature. It also seems likely that there are further severances and fusions, with their attendant traumas, to come. But this tends to confirm rather than disturb the view that the Act of Union forms the matrix of modern Irish history. At any rate, the supplemental essay which now concludes the volume is, like the rest, informed by, and cast in terms of, such a general conviction.

The original book attempted to be up to date. Its successor does not; and this for three reasons. The first is the need for an interval between what is dizzily apprehended from day to day and what is understood in some meaningful pattern or other. The other two reasons induce one to be specific about that interval, and to place the terminal point at 1972. In a double sense that year was critical in the evolution of the Anglo-Irish political relationship. On the one hand, both islands, in all their parts, then determined upon becoming members of the European Economic Community. This opened up, of course, the possibility of some eventual larger sovereignty to which the old allegiances might be subordinated. Even new sets of cultural identification became dimly discernible or at least conceivable. On the other hand, the suspension – a euphemism, as almost all believed, for the winding up – of the Northern Ireland parliament in March 1972, clearly closed a chapter in Anglo-Irish history. One is tempted to name that chapter 'the aftermath of the Act of Union' or even 'the final phase of the Act of Union'.

For although Northern Ireland attained 'Home Rule' in 1921, this did not happen because it was positively desired by any party. It happened because it was the most effective mode, in the circumstances of the day, of maintaining the Act of Union, substantially, in at least six of the thirty-two counties of Ireland. Thus, paradoxically, the inauguration of a system of indirect rule in Northern Ireland in 1921 really signified the confirmation of the British connection. By a corresponding paradox, the establishment of direct rule almost fifty-one years later really signified the weakening, and perhaps ultimately the dissolution, of the tie between Great Britain and 'Ulster'. It is true that, at the time, full political integration between the two was said to be one of the alternative future courses. But even at the moment of Stormont's suspension, this seemed improbable; and every later turn of the screw has rendered such an outcome still more unlikely. If this view of the significance of March 1972 is right, then the remnant of the Act of Union, which *eo vel alio nomine* survived 1921, died or was placed under death sentence three years ago; and in the history of that Act, 1972 is a date second only in import to 1801 or 1922 – in fact, the final entry in the ledger.

I have made few changes, and those mainly stylistic, in the original text of 1967. The consequence may be that it seems, in places, behindtimes. If so, the evil may not be unmixed. For the book was written in calm days: the current tumult was about to break, but there was then no forewarning. What was written may, therefore, bear something of the impress of a vanished age. Perhaps it innocently expressed, and hence did something to preserve, for a later period, moods and notions which have been swept already into the historian's domain. It is not often that an historian has the fortune, at once good and ill, to compose on the very eve of unforeseeable but decisive change. For all that, the happenings of the past six years have done nothing to alter materially my view of 1800–1967, and it is, accordingly, in substance re-presented. Here and there I have even retained phrases which might border on the unecumenical, politically or religiously, given the climate of today. This is partly to keep the flavour of old days, and partly because it seemed more worthy of my profession to risk anachronistic asperity than current cant.

The years 1968–73 are dealt with in a supplemental section, Chapter 7. This, as is explained below, in no sense constitutes a foray into contemporary history, but is rather an attempt to provide historical perspectives for a truer and more delicate evaluation of the recent sequence of events. It is also hoped that a brighter retrospective light may be shed by reviewing the past in terms of the new developments. Broadly speaking, this has not necessitated any changes of moment in the original text. But it has involved the reappraisal, at greater depth and with more refinement, of certain of the nineteenth- and early twentieth-century phenomena. In turn, these fresh views may be, to a degree, creatures of the time of writing, 1975. But whatever is the case with history, historians themselves cannot, from time to time, be equidistant from eternity; and, as has been suggested already, there may even be benefits in this temporality. At any rate, no matter how violent and far-reaching the changes to come in the immediate future may be, they cannot alter the patterns of two centuries out of recognition.

One other passage in the first preface seems quite as apposite now as then:

> A very small book with very large themes must assume a great deal and omit much more. It must be ruthlessly selective and not everyone – perhaps not anyone – would make the same selection as the present author. There is not space to elaborate disputed issues; one leaps boldly without the safety apparatus of marshalled evidence and corps of references. There is not time for introductory descriptions of the actors and the forces; they march upon the stage unheralded and reveal their character while on the boards. Not least, the necessity to portray the present and the immediate past bears very hard on a historian and Chapters 5 and 6 are inevitably more tentative and less balanced than the rest. They call for special charity from the critic. . . . 'Nor let us be too hard upon that just but anxious fellow that sat down dutifully to paint the soul of Switzerland upon a fan.'

To those whom I originally thanked, Mr J. M. Main, Dr J. B. O'Brien and Miss C. Cameron, I wish to add the names of Professor F. X. Martin of University College, Dublin, and Dr F. B. Smith of the Australian National University, who criticised the supplementary chapter with, I trust, their usual acuity undiminished by their personal kindness.

Finally, I acknowledge with gratitude the permission of Mr M. B. Yeats and Macmillan & Co. Ltd to reprint lines from *The Collected Works of W. B. Yeats,* and of Mr Heaney and Faber & Faber Ltd to reprint lines from Seamus Heaney's *North.*

O. MacD.
Canberra, 1975

1
The Union

With true Irish paradox, the starting point for a survey of recent Irish history can be no earlier than the Act of Union of 1800. The entire Home Rule agitation and all the nineteenth- and twentieth-century movements for parliamentary independence were conditioned by the fact that, to take legal effect, they required the repeal of this statute at Westminster. South Africa might be granted dominion status with comparative ease because the grant did not involve existing legislation, but in the Irish case the House of Lords could block the way absolutely down to 1914, because the 1800 Act could not be altered without its consent. Moreover, the Act of Union possessed for many the solemnity of fundamental law, far beyond the pretensions of ordinary legislation. With the finality of a vast constitutional rearrangement, it fenced in the range of the politically possible in the nineteenth century just as the Revolutionary Settlement of 1689 had confined eighteenth-century English politics within an ambit. We cannot understand the reactions of Unionists, British or Irish, in the years 1885–1914, unless we realise that such a view was passionately and sincerely held. Nor should we, looking back from what has actually happened, conclude that, no matter how sincerely held, this view was inherently implausible. For the groups who engrossed domestic political power in Ireland in 1800, the Union represented a surrender of valuable privileges. In return, their Protestant religion, their property, and their social domination were to be secured. Church, land, ascendancy, and equal rights of race and citizenship with their fellows in Great Britain – all these were to be saved by yielding them up to an invincible defender. We must remember that to the men of 1800 perpetual security still seemed attainable. Neither modern historiography nor the pace of modern political change, which have prepared our minds for endless whirligigs of fortune, had as yet struck the surface. It was with these dispositions, on the part of both the British and the Irish agents, that the Act of Union was formulated. Their children, actual and spiritual, inherited their sense that the statute constituted a timeless, inviolable trust.

Conversely, the Act of Union was intimately bound up with, and was in fact a direct response to, Irish nationalism. In the modern senses of the words, nationalism and republicanism in Ireland date from the 1790s. They derived from and were to some extent determined by the French revolutionary experience. The Act of Union was a deliberate counter to these phenomena; and so long as it was maintained, it was more or less threatened by the forces which had provoked its inception. It is hardly too much to say that, in the end, it was these forces or forces of the same family which contrived its destruction. Thus there is a significant organic unity in the conflict of the years 1795-1925; perhaps we might even say the years 1795-1975. This conflict deepened, extended, and intensified, not steadily, but in successive waves. Attempts to form separate kingdoms, to form a single kingdom, and to render society in the British Isles homogeneous, projects of domestic self-government, federalism, and devolution – all failed in turn and in a variety of forms. The ultimate resort to arms looked back directly to the original resort to arms a century and a quarter earlier. Whatever else changed, the wheel came full circle here. The cycle was one designated by Unionism on the one hand, and by an undying resistance to the Union and to the order which it was designed to sustain on the other.

Moreover, as Irish nationalism developed, the legality and still more the moral validity of the Act of Union were denied. It was argued that in 1800 neither parliament represented, in any acceptable sense, the peoples involved; and as popular sovereignty as the source of political authority gained in estimation in the nineteenth century, so the Act of Union became more vulnerable. Gradually, the idea of superseding the false by a legitimate Irish government took shape, and was practically expressed. Of course, the United Irishmen, deeply impregnated by the new French radicalism of the 1790s, grounded themselves on the theory that 'The People' (or rather the handful of activists who discerned and expressed their real will) were the only true government, the source of law. The United Irishmen were soon overwhelmed in a torrent of reaction and disappointment. But doctrinaire nationalism was overlaid, not killed. In the later 1840s it was re-expressed, though only vaguely and inferentially, in the Young Ireland party. But the Fenian movement, following close upon the heels of Young Ireland, deliberately revived the concept of the Irish Republic, inherent in the very existence of an Irish people; buried, unseen, by many even unsuspected, but in fact undying, indestructible, real. From 1858 to 1916 this strain was continued by the doctrinaires of the nationalist movements, and reached its apotheosis in the Proclamation of a Republic in Easter Week 1916. Patrick Pearse did not consider that he was inventing independent government for Ireland. He believed that he was 'asserting in arms' and attempting to make palpable a truth implicit in the very existence of an Irish nation.

Parallel with this theoretical repudiation of the Act of Union there developed, pragmatically, various campaigns which sought to undercut the existing government and provide a substitute from below. The first indication of what was to come was perhaps the Catholic Association's development, in 1826–8, of pacificatory and other instruments of social control. The first unambiguous move in the same direction was, however, Patrick Lalor's attempt in 1831 to organise a conscientious, though pacific, resistance by the Catholics to meeting their legal obligation to pay tithes to the Anglican Church in Ireland, even if this involved the seizure of their possessions (a tactic used by English dissenters, anti-vaccinationists and others with very considerable effect later in the century). Lalor's activity contained the embryo of civil disobedience which was to be fully grown in the Land League's 'No Rent Manifesto' and the Plan of Campaign in the 1880s. Particularly in this last, the fixing, collection and distribution of rents were organised by the tenants and their leaders, the ordinary agencies of law enforcement being quite set aside. Sinn Fein (Ourselves Alone), initiated by Arthur Griffith in 1905, rationalised and generalised the strategy. Assuming the illegality of 'British rule' – because the Act of Union was illegal – it looked forward to the development of indigenous organs of government which would quietly come to provide the order currently imposed by an alien, illegitimate power. The British state in Ireland would wither away as the native Irish state took form. In some respects, Griffith's work strongly resembled Robert Owen's New Moral Order, which was to come into being by the spontaneous regeneration of the industrial structure, cell by cell. But Sinn Fein was more than 'visionary'. In the event, a vital force in securing the independence of 1921 was the complex of loan raising, revenue distribution, local government, legal adjudication and enforcement and general sovereignty, set up in Ireland in defiance of the ordinary modes of government, which were in part superseded.

Much of the story of Irish resistance and discontent, therefore, centres upon notions and stratagems which defied the Act of Union. 'The Act of Union', Griffith wrote in 1902, 'was at the time of its passage and has always since been declared by independent Irish lawyers and Irish statesmen to be a nullity, a usurpation and a fraud.

... And the practice of sending Irishmen to represent the Irish people in an Imperial Parliament is an acquiescence in a usurpation and a fraud.' Almost all the Irish agitators would have accepted the first assertion, and even those devoted to parliamentary means would probably have justified their membership of the House of Commons as mere tactics.

The Act of Union was, like much other legislation, an act of miscalculations. Born of fears – of French invasion, of revolution, of social levelling, and of what a frightened peasantry or an embattled and hysterical ruling class might undertake in terror – it appeared to offer a release on every side from current pressures. To the British government, it promised to close a dangerous gap in national defence and to furnish a solution to what was already an Irish Question. The population of Ireland, comprising one-third of the inhabitants of the British Isles, was three-quarters 'disaffected'. Incorporation, or at least containment within a single kingdom, seemed more practicable than outright subjection, all the more so as the safeguard of religious discrimination was weakening year by year. To the Protestant 'nation' in Ireland, the Union promised an end to the blood-red nightmare of a jacquerie. After the Wexford rising of 1798, most Irish Protestants believed with Cooke, Pitt's undersecretary, 'Ireland is like a ship on fire, it must either be extinguished or cut adrift': at all costs, therefore, they must be fastened to Great Britain. Moreover, their experience since 1782 had suggested that concessions to Catholics could not be, or at least would not be, indefinitely postponed. A movement toward civil equality was the drift of history. If Catholic political participation were inevitable, should it not be neutralised by taking place within a system in which the Catholic participants would constitute a small minority instead of potential masters? To the Irish Catholic episcopate and to the main, moderate body of educated lay Catholics, the Union promised, immediately and with no dangerous violence, their prime objective, political and civil emancipation. Less palpably but perhaps as certainly, it also seemed an antidote to the fevers of doctrinaire republicanism and infidelity. These were the predominant calculations. The bulk of the well-to-do Irish Anglicans and Catholics, and even a majority of the Ulster Presbyterians, probably favoured the Union as a *pis aller* at the time of its inception. The parliamentary opposition to the measure must not be taken at its full face value. Some of the reluctance to accept the measure is attributable to bargaining for money, honours and place; and much of the 'bribery' and 'corruption' which eased the passage of the Bill was, in contemporary eyes, mere compensation for the loss of political or administrative 'property'.

The provisions of the Act of Union involved similar miscalculations. Cooke assured Pitt, 'By giving the Irish one hundred members in an assembly of 650 they will be rendered impotent to operate in that assembly, but it will be invested with Irish assent to its authority'. A century later it was clear that precisely the opposite had happened. With the development of a party system in Great Britain, even a small independent group, if disciplined, could exercise a degree of influence altogether disproportionate to its numbers; and Parliament proved a most effective medium for advertising the fact that the majority of its decisions were not invested with Irish assent. As Cobden once said, when one speaks in the House of Commons one uses a very long whip. With 100 members, moreover, Ireland was grossly under-represented in 1800 in terms of population. But by 1900, with 105 members, she was grossly over-represented; and such was the Irish Party's power by then that this over-representation was practically inviolable, into the bargain. The Church of Ireland was guaranteed 'forever' – 'forever' was a sort of incantation in the Act – its ecclesiastical supremacy, its corporate property, and its traditional tithe income, by virtue of the complete unity of church and state in the new polity. Within seventy years, all these had been torn down, notwithstanding the desperate assertions of their defenders that the Union had rendered them eternal.

Whether or not the financial provision of the Act, which saddled Ireland with two-seventeenths of the national expenditure, represented a reasonable obligation is a nice and perhaps unanswerable question. But the expenses of holding down Irish discontent, of relieving Irish hunger, and of attempting to buy Irish quietude by economic reorganisations were certainly unforeseen. Conversely, what perhaps ultimately determined the ruin of the Irish economy, the establishment of a free trade area within the British Isles, followed by the rapid abandonment of protection for that area from external competition, was altogether unanticipated in 1800.

In keeping with these miscalculations, the retention or otherwise of the viceregal system of rule in Ireland was not discussed, let alone determined, in 1800. The lord-lieutenancy simply drifted on until it was taken to be permanent. *A fortiori*, the change which the Union would make in the position of the viceroy's main subordinate was not anticipated. The new independence of the Irish chief secretary – he was now appointed by the prime minister instead of by the viceroy, and was in general more powerful politically than the viceroy and more commonly a member of the cabinet – produced a curious dualism in Irish government, the effects of which were hardly understood, still less allowed for, in the nineteenth century. Moreover, the long-term administrative implications of the Union could scarcely have been guessed by its architects. The direct exercise of power from London and the fact that significant decisions were made there also implied that the direct responsibility was now West-minster's; and that British values and criteria would sooner or later be imposed on Ireland, and sooner or later would be themselves profoundly influenced by the Irish experience. What was meant to issue in a compound of government produced an unending series of explosions.

If the miscalculations in the Act itself were serious, the abandon-ment of the tacit understandings which produced its passage was fundamental. The decay of the underlying presuppositions of the Union provides the staple of nineteenth-century Irish history. For 'the Protestant nation', the first warranty of the contract was their continued monopoly, or at least their effective control, of local government and the public service, of the professions and higher education, of land ownership and the instruments of order. To this we might add, as a second warranty, the maintenance of the privi-leges, honorary and material, of the Established Church. For although initially, and always theoretically, the Irish non-conformists opposed church privileges as strenuously as did the Catholics, when the crisis came they put the common interests of Protestantism above any gains to be secured by joining forces with the papists.

The third warranty seemed at first self-evident. Only when the others were broken, piece by piece, did direct British government of the island, and the engrossment of legislative authority by West-minster, come to seem a matter of life and death to the Protestant nation. Perhaps we should now say Protestant nations, to allow for the very real differences between north and south: to apply the gibe about French deputies, two Ulster Protestants, only one of whom was an Anglican, had perhaps more in common than two Irish Anglicans only one of whom lived in Ulster. Paradoxically, each of these nations combined with Unionism a sense of separate Irish identity. To northern Protestants Ulster stood in essentially the same sort of relationship to the remainder of the kingdom as did Scotland after 1707: more than a province, less than a state, it constituted at least a people. The other resident Irish Protestants thought of the towns and countrysides about them as their artefacts. The noble houses, the tamed land, the canals and commerce were, to them, the fruit of their own toil, money and design. It is hardly extravagant to identify their attitudes with those of the Kenya settlers to the White Highlands. Yet this very consciousness of being British, yet more than British, this very Irishness of feeling, fed the resistance of the Protestant nations to what seemed to them to threaten their standing and locale. As they themselves cried out, Home Rule was

Rome Rule; Tenant Right was Landlord Wrong; the March of Independence was the Flight of Capital. Ireland was their home; but how could they live there except as masters? And as the retreating Protestant forces fell back, so their last bastion, the political Union, grew in significance. In the final forty years, 1880–1920, the critical struggle centred on this third great warranty.

In fact, the hundred years from 1815 to 1914 was a period of slow corrosion of the Unionist position. On the surface it might appear that little ground was lost until the later stages of the nineteenth century, although thenceforward the decline was swift. But a catastrophic interpretation would be misleading. In reality, the latest events of this period represented the culmination of nearly a century of piecemeal, ill-perceived decay. We have observed above that one of the effects of the Act of Union was to transfer political responsibility to Westminster. Even in 1800 there were probably significant differences between London and Dublin in the idea of what this responsibility implied. By 1815 the differences were certainly marked and growing fast. A new type of public servant and of public service was emerging. Administration was gradually being divorced from politics, and the notion that the state should stand outside and above the contending groups and parties was taking shape. It took, of course, many decades before this revolution was complete, all the more so because the change was unplanned and unpremeditated. But, unmistakably, it was under way even in the first quarter of the nineteenth century; and from the start this development was most rapid and most radical in Ireland. Even in Sir Robert Peel's Irish secretaryship (1812–18) the outlines of the new order can be discerned. Peel was then the unbending opponent of Catholic emancipation, of constitutional and parliamentary reform, and of the repeal of the Act of Union. Yet he would not serve as the instrument of mere orangeism, giving the spoils to the eternal victors in the Irish contests without regard to the social and moral consequences. His passions for economy, efficiency and a 'science' of society led him, willy-nilly, toward neutrality in his dealings with the disparate elements of a turbulent island. He himself declared in 1816 that 'an honest despotic Government would be by far the fittest government for Ireland'. The trouble was that 'honesty' and 'despotism' were ceasing to be compatible by British standards. It was, of course, in keeping with Peel's own disposition to abhor the feeling that he was being made the tool of faction. But Irish circumstances were sufficiently foreign to the other English and Scottish administrators involved in Irish government to induce most of them to take up substantially the same position. Few would identify themselves with the squireens, the rake-hellies, the shabby genteel, the office jobbers, the rack-renters and the rash apostles of the New Reformation who provided the most immediate, if by no means the most important, manifestations of Irish Protestantism.

Once he stood apart from factions and started to look upon the privileged sections not as the bulwark of civilisation but as a party, the public servant naturally tended to regard himself as umpire or adjudicator. This effect was especially marked where the administrator was either a deliberate 'reformer' or a practical man with technical knowledge and desiderata. When, for example, Thomas Drummond, Irish undersecretary from 1835 to 1840, sought to improve the administration of justice, or when Sir John Burgoyne, the chairman of the reconstituted Irish Board of Works from 1831, sought to build and drain and level in the interests of the entire economy, they were soon in conflict with the magistrates, proprietors and general influence which barred the way. Of course, the development of a principle of impartiality was not uniform or steady throughout all branches of the Irish government. There were ebbs and flows in sympathy with the variations in British policy. 'Cold warriors' could be found in Dublin Castle in every phase. Yet overall we can say that the concept of the neutral and impartial state began to take root in the Irish system before 1830, and grew astonishingly in several fields before 1845.

The growth of this concept was, of course, assisted by the changes in the structure and spirit of English politics, especially after 1830. Anglican power was weakened by the repeal of the Test and Corporation Acts in 1828, by the enlargement of the lower-middle-class electorate in 1832, and by the secular character of the new forms of local government thrown up by the Poor Law Amendment Act of 1834, and by the Municipal Reform Act of 1835. Side by side with the advances in civil equality and non-conformist influence, the pace of 'economical reform', directed against the old order of family connection and jobbing in public offices, quickened. 'A placeman is in these days an odious animal,' confessed poor Charles Greville in 1834, 'and as a double placeman I am doubly odious'. When this wind of change blew across St George's Channel, as was inevitable with a single parliament and a single cabinet for a single kingdom, it struck directly at Protestant power in Ireland, inextricably connected, as it was, with the *ancien régime*. With all this, the breaking of the warranties began.

The weakest sector of the Protestant front was that which relied directly upon religious discrimination. Both the *Zeitgeist* and the shifts in political power in Great Britain in the first half of the nineteenth century worked steadily against Anglican privilege; it was only to be expected that the earliest losses should have been suffered in this region. Of course, these losses had repercussions beyond the strict confines of religion. The first and greatest loss, the Catholic Emancipation Act of 1829, attempted to strike away O'Connell's popular support by substituting a ten-pound for a forty-shilling freehold as the property qualification for enfranchisement, and not merely to exclude Catholics from the highest offices of state, but also to penalise them by proscribing religious orders and any public demonstration of faith, such as the wearing of clerical habits out of doors. But Catholic political power was only diminished, not destroyed; and the new penal clauses against religion were a dead-letter: no government would have dared to place hundreds of monks, friars and nuns in the dock. The Irish Poor Law of 1838 weighted the franchise for the new organs of local government in favour of the well-to-do, and left the essentially Protestant grand juries with considerable powers. But at least no bar to Catholic membership of the boards of guardians was imposed. Similarly, the Irish Municipal Reform Act of 1840 was meagre in contrast to the English legislation of 1835. Yet once again an Anglican monopoly was breached. Technically the Church of Ireland was now on a level with the rest in local government, and in fact most of the Irish corporations were captured by the nationalist or Catholic interests. Beginning with Daniel O'Connell's election as Lord Mayor of Dublin in 1841, this represented an indirect but not inconsiderable change in the structure of city politics.

Apart from these palpable Catholic advances, Protestant influence was gradually receding in society at large. In part, the change consisted in the opening to native Catholics of some of the old offices, and more in the new departments of government. This trend set in in the 1830s when the Whig-Liberal cabinets angled for Irish support, and state activity commenced in several virgin fields. In part, the silent transformation grew out of increased Catholic participation in the professions and in the higher range of mercantile and petty manufacturing activity. All this was still a far cry from equality of standing and opportunity. Protestants were still predominant in Ireland in 1850. But by then their predominance was neither as substantial nor as secure as it had been a half, or even a quarter, of a century before.

It was even more difficult for the Anglicans to maintain the hegemony of an Established Church in Ireland than to repel the Catholics clamouring against personal disabilities. British non-conformity was positively eager to destroy Anglican privilege the world over, where it merely favoured – and that doubtfully – civic equality for the Catholics. Meanwhile, 'Churchmen' were forced to undertake an agonising reappraisal in the 1830s. The strains upon the concept of a spiritually homogeneous society, with the Established Church claiming a universal allegiance, grew so rapidly that the theory came to appear totally unreal. Of course, the sudden addition of 5 million Irish Catholics to the United Kingdom was a precipitant of the crisis: here, as in so many places, the Act of Union recoiled completely. 'The state', Newman told Gladstone in 1845, 'has a thousand consciences. That is to say, it has no conscience'; and Gladstone was perhaps the last man to leave (which he did in the same year) the sinking ship of one-religion-for-one-polity.

Political changes both fed and were fed by the shift in concepts. The system of national elementary education set up in Ireland in 1831 was, in theory, non-denominational, or rather supra-denominational. The fact that Catholics came later to quarrel with its Protestant content as well as with its secularism should not blind us to the revolutionary character of a vast national undertaking, on the basis of religious neutrality, only thirty years after the Act of Union. Correspondingly, although Peel's 'Godless Colleges' of 1845 were anathematised by the Catholic bishops as nurseries of infidelity, the 'infidelity' was aimed at by none. Once again, it was the product of the state's abandonment or mitigation of the policy of privilege for Protestants, or, more precisely, Anglicans. The suppression of two archbishoprics and eight bishoprics of the Church of Ireland in 1833 may have driven Pusey to fire a shot which rang around the English-speaking world. But Pusey's shot did not change the legislation: the secular power had ruthlessly reordered the ecclesiastical economy. The tithe issue which spluttered on throughout the 1830s presented the Established Church in Ireland in its least defensible role. A peasantry on the border of starvation was paying the bulk of a tax which supported a religion, hostile and aggressive toward their own: all Irishmen were forced to contribute to a church to which less than 15 per cent of the population belonged. The transference, by the Tithe Commutation Act of 1838, of the obligation to pay tithes from the occupier to the owner of land often may have meant merely that the owner recovered the amount by raising the rent proportionately. But another Anglican 'principle' had been broken; and the Church of Ireland, summoning military forces to collect its dues amidst ragged crowds and burning hovels, had presented a cruel spectacle to the world. The way was being prepared for disestablishment.

The Disestablishment Act of 1869 was far from being the spoliation of which the Conservatives accused Gladstone. About three-quarters of the endowment, some £13·5 million (over £100 million in present values), was given over absolutely to the Church of Ireland. Yet the hard facts remained that the last quarter was distributed by the state for various secular objects, and that the Church of Ireland had lost forever its formal pre-eminence and its status as representative of the Crown. Except for the social cachet attached to its membership and the (in Irish terms) vast wealth of its adherents, it was no longer even *primus inter pares* among Irish churches. It had been cut back almost to its irreducible essence: to serve as the chaplaincy of a garrison. So much had been lost since 1801; and the very bitterness of the Anglican resistance to reform meant that the defeat of 1869 had ulterior consequences. The long struggle had kept the Catholic Church in or near the centre of Irish politics. It had tended to entwine religion with party, to widen – if that were possible – the chasm between the sects. Most important of all, slowly, imperceptibly, but surely, it had identified Catholicism with nationality.

'The pope one day and potatoes the next.' Disraeli's epitome of the Irish Question had some point. If, generally speaking, it was the religious grievances which were most widely canvassed down to 1850, it was agrarian grievances which dominated the second half of the century. No sooner had the religious warranty finally disappeared in 1869, than the social and economic warranty was undermined by the Irish Land Act of 1870. The position of the landed proprietors had deteriorated markedly during and immediately after the Great Famine of 1845–52. But this was a natural process, certainly unaccompanied by any official endeavour to improve the relative standing of the tenants. If Parliament had done little to restore the fortunes of the original proprietors between 1845 and 1865, it had done something to shore up the proprietorial system. The Encumbered Estates Act of 1849 and Deasy's and Cardwell's Acts of 1860 had tried to promote the English form of capitalist landowning by easing the transference of title and rendering tenancy agreements more contractual. But the 1870 Act marked the turning of the tide. Of itself, it was ineffectual in weakening the actual power of the actual proprietors; nor did its authors intend this result. But it did symbolise a defeat for the traditional concept of land ownership. Up to this stage, ownership in Ireland was conceived of as both absolute and free from obligations, social or specific, to the tenants. In fact, most Irish landlords were circumspect in enforcing their 'rights' in the 1850s and 1860s. But however much their practices were informed by prudence, their theories were unyielding. The 1870 Act, as we shall see, sold the pass in the realm of concepts even if it did little immediately to improve the tenant's lot.

Apart from this initial and ambiguous concession, the 1870s produced another critical decision on the agrarian issue, this time by a Conservative government. Disraeli's ministry refused to protect British agriculture from foreign competition during the disastrous harvests of 1877–9, even though the domestic difficulties were aggravated by a new flood of cereals from overseas. The Conservatives had fixed all their attention upon the British urban electorates and ignored the example of the various Continental governments who met the same problem by either introducing or augmenting agricultural protection. More to the point, the Conservatives ignored not only the British but also the Irish farmers. This had two very significant results. On the one hand, it provided the motive power for the countrywide civil disobedience of the years 1879–82 and for the welding of the Irish party into a single effective weapon. On the other, it broke the morale of many of the Irish landowners, who, especially after the further failures and redoubled agitation of 1885–6, saw a vista of falling prices, failing rents and rural turbulence opening out on to final ruin. Without such an experience, the passage of measures of land purchase for redistribution to the occupiers would have been much more difficult. But, with this experience, many proprietors were at least resigned, or even compliant, in being bought out and having their capital investment transferred to safer regions. There is a neat irony here, as in so many aspects of nineteenth-century Irish history. Had it not been for a Malthusian catastrophe such as the Great Famine, and its aftermath, a declining population, the density of population would have been too great for peasant proprietorship to have been established; and had it not been for the agricultural disasters of 1877–9 and 1885–6 the existing proprietary might not have been dislodged without a bloody conflict of vast dimensions.

The Land Act of 1881 recognised explicitly the revolutionary principles half expressed in the 1870 measure. In effect, it admitted a degree of co-ownership in the landlord-tenant relationship and attempted to satisfy the stock demand of the Irish agrarian agitators for more than a generation, the celebrated '3 Fs', fixity of tenure, fair rent and free sale. The turnabout in the concept of property rights begun in 1870 and completed in 1881 seriously weakened the landlord's position. But if the Liberals had brought the proprietors to their knees, it was the Conservatives who facilitated their removal from the scene with a series of land purchase measures, beginning with Ashbourne's Act of 1885 and culminating in Wyndham's Act of 1903. Simultaneously, the Conservative reforms of Irish local government reduced landlord influence in this sphere to negligible proportions. We should not treat these final blows as an instant surrender of 'The Night of the Fourth of August' type. The change in the ownership of land worked slowly over four decades, and even at the end the surviving ex-proprietors retained much of their social power. But the last decades of the nineteenth century did mark the

beginning of the end of the economic privilege and the near monopoly of landed wealth which the Act of Union had seemed to
guarantee 'forever'. Meanwhile, the first really dangerous assault
upon the Union itself, Parnell's, was already under way.

As a shadowy overlay upon this basic pattern of conflict, the
attempts to escape from the bare alternatives of defence and offence
also deserve attention – all the more so as historians, obsessed with
the final outcome, have neglected these unrealised possibilities. Could
the common interests of the Irish protagonists at any stage have so
outweighed the divisive factors as to produce a viable compromise?
Broadly, the matter divides into three. First, the possibilities of
Catholic Unionism. The Union had been enacted with Catholic
support, and although the failure to grant emancipation for almost
thirty years and the offensive form of the surrender had alienated
Irish Catholicism, British governments continued to back this forlorn
hope for most of the remainder of the nineteenth century. Three
factors favoured it: the papacy; the offices and emoluments at the
disposal of governments; and the desire of many Catholics, high or
rising in the economic scale, to enter the charmed circle of society.
But these forces were quite insufficient to outweigh their opposites.
The political domination of O'Connell in the first half of the century
fixed the connections between the Church and popular agitation, and
anti-Unionism. The next two decades offered better prospects, now
that there was a well-beaten track leading Irish Catholics to judicial
and other offices, and an increasing danger that Irish nationalism
would become identified with conspiracy, violence and anti-
clericalism. But even in 1850–70 Catholic Unionism was a will-o'-the-
wisp. Except for a handful of extremists in either case, the Irish
hierarchy continued to reject the British connection, and the Fenians
to number themselves privately amongst the faithful. Moreover, the
number of Catholics who could enter the Garrison by the bridges of
judgeships or attendance at viceregal levees was very small, while
British ministries could never press the cause of Catholic concession
too hard in the face of English, not to add Irish, Protestant hostility.
What finally destroyed all prospects for this form of 'reconciliation'
was the democratisation of the franchise and the creation of a
powerful Home Rule party in the early 1880s. Entrance to Parliament
in Catholic Ireland was henceforth contingent upon a specific
repudiation of the Union, and an involvement in a serious and
ceaseless struggle for its overthrow. Moreover, the Catholic community was by now substantially established, and Unionism palpably
in decline in terms of real power.

The next type of possible junction was the opposite one: a
coalition of the underprivileged in both religious communions.

Indeed, in the first three-quarters of the nineteenth century the prospects of combined operations between the northern Presbyterians and the Catholic masses seemed fair. In three major areas of politics, the issues of land tenure, of Anglican privilege and of working-class needs, the demands of the two converged. One movement in particular, the Tenant Right agitation of the early 1850s, was deliberately based upon an alliance for economic ends between north and south. But the collapse of that agitation, broken, partly at least, by religious dissension, signalised that sectarianism had not diminished since 1800. In fact, it had increased. Other fleeting, tantalising prospects of a common front opened in later years, the most remarkable belonging to the first decade of the twentieth century. A breakaway movement among the Protestant working class in Belfast, another among the Protestant small farmers of the north-east and yet another aiming ostensibly at a revival in Ulster of the eighteenth-century objective of dual monarchy, struck the surface together in 1900–5. But all three proved flimsy contrivances, easily borne down by the gale of ferocious Unionism which sprang up with the apparent imminence of Home Rule after 1906. The truth is that the history of Ulster's relations with the rest of Ireland under the Act of Union was one of growing antipathy: or perhaps we should regard the antipathy as fixed, but only gradually revealed, as the power of the Catholic masses increased and serious projects of political combination could be devised. Certainly the fate of the Tenant Right movement, of the simultaneous association of Ulster non-conformist and Catholic political organisations with the Liberal Party in the 1860s and 1870s, and of the Dungannon Clubs a generation later bear this out, while the Orange delirium of 1885–6, 1891–2 and 1911–14 seems to establish finally that the essential disposition of Ulster Protestants toward Irish independence was one of unconquerable distrust.

The history of the Unionists in the remaining three provinces of Ireland is curiously contrasting. As the Protestant solidarity of Ulster and its self-identification with the Union became clearer in the last quarter of the nineteenth century, the ascendancy in the south began to show signs of fissures and reappraisals. It would be too much to regard the years 1885–1918 as an era of repentant landlordism, for the great majority of southern Unionists were immovable. But a sufficient number reconsidered their position to alter – or at least to promise to alter – the course of Anglo-Irish history. First, there was always a Protestant and proprietorial element in the Home Rule party; in fact, its first three leaders were Protestant, and even to the end the proportion of Protestants among the Nationalist members of Parliament was significantly higher than the proportion of Protestants in the Nationalist constituencies. Moreover, after 1910 a considerable number joined the radical, separatist wing of the independence movement. The Howth gun-running of 1914, which made practicable the 1916 rebellion, was entirely managed by ex-Unionists; and two of them, Erskine Childers and Robert Barton, played critical parts in producing the split in 1922. The presence of this Protestant element in the anti-British movements ensured that Irish nationalism in the south adhered to its theoretical non-sectarianism, so far as might reasonably have been expected in a most unpromising situation.

This headlong identification with the Irish mass movements created a chasm between the relatively small section of the ascendancy which took this step and the large majority of southern Unionists. The main body would not 'capitulate' simply to their hereditary subjects. But was some *aggiornamento*, some reconciliation of interests at a new level, quite impossible? Superimposed upon the customary Irish conflict, the chance of a *détente* and of a fresh beginning was faintly discernible from the middle 1890s to the closing stages of the First World War. In part, this represented a recognition that Irishmen of every type had certain common interests. Initially, all could freely unite behind the claim in 1895 that Ireland had been overtaxed relative to the remainder of the United Kingdom since 1801, and the demand for proportionate compensation. At first sight, the next stage, the systematic improvement of Irish primary production by state loans, scientific investigation, technical education and the co-operative employment of modern machinery and joint purchasing and marketing, seemed equally unexceptional. The third stage, the peaceful solution of the land question, might also have seemed so patently in the general interest that none would have preferred the continuation of the destructive struggle.

Yet this movement for the supra-political settlement of matters which it was to everyone's economic advantage to resolve encountered covert opposition on either wing even before the Land Conference of 1902 brought about an open conflagration. On the Unionist side the reason for the opposition, headed by diehards such as Lord Ardilaun, was a resuscitation of ancient fears, suspicions and contempt, the counterpart in fact of the violent Tory reaction in Great Britain to the threatened social revolution in 1909–13. The nationalist opposition was more complicated. First came the traditional distrust of 'our hereditary oppressors'; for obvious reasons, this was especially marked amongst Ulster Catholics. More important was the fact that the conciliation movement developed under a Unionist regime. Between 1886 and 1890 Parnell's entire strategy was based upon the Liberal alliance, which also constituted the very *raison d'être* of the anti-Parnellite Party from 1891 to 1900. Certain dominant Nationalists, chief among them the anti-Parnellite John Dillon, continued to assume that Home Rule could only be achieved through a Liberal government, and that consequently the simple and necessary duty of the Irish Party was to oppose all Unionist reforms, whatever short-term advantages they might seem to offer. Thirdly – and again Dillon was the foremost adherent of the view – it was argued that ameliorisation in Ireland would blunt the edge of nationalist agitation. For a quarter of a century economic and especially agrarian grievances had provided the driving force of the parliamentary movement for independence; hence it followed (though even Dillon might have hesitated to put it quite so bluntly) that the Irish farmer's gain was the Irish nation's loss – at least until Home Rule was safely gathered in.

Although the opponents of conciliation had become increasingly uneasy at the trend toward agreement since the Local Government Act of 1898, it was the successful Land Conference of 1902 which proved the breaking point. Landlord and tenant representatives at the conference had agreed upon a scheme for establishing peasant proprietorship on a basis of state loans and grants to cover the difference between what the landlords were prepared to sell for and the tenants were prepared to pay. The Unionist government accepted the agreement substantially and embodied it in the Land Act of 1903. Two features of this reconciliation – the use of public money to smooth the way of reform, and the frank avowal of co-operation between the classes (in this case the conference asked that the landlords, though expropriated, should not be expelled from but rather cherished in Ireland) – had been basic elements of the policy of 'enlightenment' from 1895 onwards. Secret, and then open, resistance within the Nationalist Party, and die-hardism among the proprietors, soon developed. Ultimately, what moved both of these sections was the future of the Union. Each saw gradualist conciliation ending in an unacceptable agreement on the government of Ireland. Certainly, the moderates in each camp were looking forward to the eventual negotiation of the Union issue, and it was the first tentative step in this direction which brought their dreams crashing about their heads.

In the autumn of 1904 a group of moderate Unionists, the Irish Reform Association, proposed an attempt at a peaceful solution of the constitutional issue. Both sets of traditionalists seized their opportunity not merely to discredit conciliation, lock, stock and barrel, but also to render the Land Act unworkable, by extravagant demands and renewed hostility, over most areas of the country. Conciliation was not yet quite dead, but circumstances of equal promise never recurred. The Unionist Party went out of power in 1905 and did not return to office until after the growth of violence in Ireland had ruined the cause of peaceful settlement. As William O'Brien, the leading 'conciliator' among the Nationalists, noted prophetically early in the century, the conference method offered the only escape, short of war, from the impasses created by the capacities of both Orange Ulster and the House of Lords to wreck Home Rule; and, even if the conference method were attempted, only a Conservative ministry could hope to induce either of these enemies to abate its resistance. All of the attempts after 1905 to break the deadlock by means of conference were of a different character from the 1895–1903 efforts to reach a compromise. They sprang, not from an Irish initiative, but from the despair of British cabinets; and they aimed immediately at shelving or smothering, rather than solving, the Irish problem.

None the less, the last of these efforts, the Irish Convention of 1917–18, was remarkably revealing on the drift of the southern Unionists toward the Nationalist camp, and away from their northern brethren. At the Convention, the intransigent Nationalists stood out for genuine and immediate autonomy in internal matters, and for the withdrawal of Irish members from Westminster. The Ulster intransigents rightly discerned in this the assertion of a natural right to self-government on the ground of separate nationality. Logically, from their point of view, they refused to move from the existing Union, which sufficiently repudiated and protected them from such a political philosophy. But the southern Unionist representatives at the Convention tried to pursue both objects simultaneously. Apart from some reservations on Ireland's fiscal independence (to protect their own economic interests), they agreed to recommend a measure of self-government which went far beyond the original Home Rule demands of either Parnell or his ultimate successor as leader of the parliamentary party, John Redmond. On the other hand, they spoke of continued Irish representation in the British Parliament as indispensable. In short, they had come to express, and were now prepared to accept, their double affinity in a radically new form which attempted to serve the causes of separate nationality and of the Union together. As Dr Leo Kohn wrote of this, 'It was a position untenable in itself, yet characteristically indicative of a new realistic orientation that was soon to reshape the traditional alignment of political parties in Ireland'. Was the dualism necessarily impracticable? Certainly it was in 1918, by which time the main body of Irish feeling had settled on principles of self-determination and separation, whose other face was abhorrence of the British connection. But one could not say this with equal confidence of 1908, still less of 1903, least of all of 1886. However, the half-conversion of southern Unionism was much too late, not to say too limited to the most advanced and perceptive members of that class, to affect the issue by the closing stages of the First World War.

Thus the faint counter-theme of conciliation faded. The Union recovered and retained its dubious distinction as *the* Irish Question. That this should have been the case in the first two decades of the present century may well appear a scandal to 'materialist' and 'realist' historians. But so it was. By now the conflict had been practically reduced – or rather refined – to one of bare feeling, of elemental antipathy and sympathy. After all, what had Great Britain really to fear from home rule or dominion status or even a Republic of Ireland after 1900? The surrender of a strategic centre, of a necessary defence against invasion, of Atlantic bases? Later events were to establish that even the more extreme Republicans were prepared to accommodate Great Britain on this issue, for her concern for naval and military security was accepted as understandable. It might of course be a question whether, say, British airfields in Ireland, or a British guaranteed neutrality for Ireland, would be compatible in their eyes with essential independence. But even such matters were probably negotiable. There was no final, irreconcilable conflict of interests in this field. Did – to repeat another notion familiar at the time – Great Britain really fear that the Irish were incapable of governing themselves, and that she might find herself flanked by a Latin-American type of instability if she withdrew? Again events were to prove that in the long run no fear was more groundless; if anything, the fault was too faithful a reproduction of the parent's stolidity. To plead absence-of-wisdom-before-the-event to justify this English misapprehension would also involve, in logic, a refusal to allow any race without self-government to attain it.

What of Great Britain's concern for free trade within the British Isles and financial control of the entire area? In theory an independent Ireland, by very definition, would possess the right to pursue divergent and even antagonistic economic and fiscal policies. But the reality was of course quite different. The Irish had no access, in a significant degree, to alternative export markets; to break with sterling would have been pointless as well as impracticable; and it was obviously Ireland which would suffer first and most in any tariff war between the two islands. In this field, too, Great Britain had little to lose from conceding formal independence – at any rate, in the conditions prevailing in the first quarter of the twentieth century.

This left the most powerful if the least substantiated fear of all – the fear of religious persecution or discrimination by Irish Catholics, accompanied perhaps by the spoliation of Irish Protestant property. Here the gap between what was feared and what actually happened was perhaps greatest of all. The principal deprivation (if they so regarded it) of Protestants in the Irish Free State was psychological – the sense of separation, in deep matters of feeling and belief, from the bulk of the community in which they lived. Against this, some were doubtless compensated psychologically by the sense of social irresponsibility and superiority which a small, privileged and prized minority inevitably enjoys. Otherwise, their collective economic resources remained, and still remain, wildly in excess of their proportionate numbers in the population; and, so far from being shut out from, they are cosseted (and only partly as an advertisement of toleration) in public life. True, Protestants (perhaps others, too) may have been outraged by the use of the new state's powers to enforce censorship and prohibit contraception and divorce. But their material disadvantages under this head were confined, even in the 1920s, to additional inconvenience and expense in procuring what they wanted. So much for the religious issue.

Ultimately, then, the opposition to Irish self-government in the first decades of the present century had little material or even rational foundation. (Of course, if the desire to govern oneself is not accepted as rational *per se*, the equivalent would be true of the advocacy of Irish independence; but, as Shaw observed, a nationalist movement 'is only the agonising symptom of a suppressed natural function'.) The groundlessness of the arguments against Irish separation by no means implies that they were insincere. But it does suggest that they were, in some degree, mere ancestral shibboleths and rationalisations of a deeper impulse. In fact, this was so. What finally divided the two sides were the symbols representing the acceptance or the repudiation of subordination to Great Britain. In British eyes, hatred of Crown and empire was a mortal and inexplicable offence. It affronted pride, made sudden and inordinate demands upon the political imagination, and called on conscience to acknowledge that past acquisition and present power were wrong. To Irishmen, Crown and empire were by now the very badges of their inferiority. Their historical view had crystallised into something simple and negative: simple because they imposed upon the past an undifferentiating pattern of oppression and resistance; negative because their conception of liberty was the absence of specific existing claims and institutions. On both counts, the symbols of British authority had become unendurable in themselves.

In its last phase, then, it was the pure principle, the very idea, of the Act of Union, and not its substantial clauses, which was at stake. But this idea, so lightly taken up in 1800, bred perhaps the greatest tragedies in all its history in the year of its formal abandonment,

1920, and the immediate aftermath. At least, such seemed to be the case. Now, it appears, we no longer know tragedy's limit. As Heaney's 'Act of Union' sadly concludes,

> . . . No treaty
> I foresee will salve completely your tracked
> And stretchmarked body . . .

2
The Siamese Twins

Between 1800 and 1920 Ireland was, for most practical purposes, a political dependency. Although formally part of the same state, she was not and could not have been ruled in the same fashion as Great Britain. Yet to rule her in a different fashion made a mockery of the Act of Union. The need to treat Ireland as a subordinate collided constantly with the policy of converting her into a component of an integrated society in the British Isles. It also vitiated the policy of converting Irishmen into outer Britons. These cross-purposes, strikingly manifested in Anglo-Irish relations, also characterised, more or less, Britain's relations with all her other dependencies at the time. An examination of the actual working of the metropolitan-colonial link in any particular case would show how little it can be explained in simple terms of power and separate entities. Instead of an impervious master and a half-conforming, half-rebellious slave, we would find that each party was modified by the inter-relationship between the two. Ireland in 1914 was largely a British product. But had the wish of the anonymous English patriot, who asked that the unhappy island be sunk below the sea for just twenty-four hours, been granted in 1815, the Britain of 1914 would have been an unrecognisably different nation.

The Union of 1801 was meant to be a union of churches, finance, administration, and political forms and participants. But no one saw it as a problem of uniting the masses. This was perhaps natural: 'society' was still thought of, essentially, as that fraction of the population which was literate, propertied and articulate. On such a view, the difficulties of a junction did not seem very great. Irish 'society' could plausibly be regarded as English society writ small. But as the nineteenth century progressed, and previously submerged classes and interests were pressed upward into view, the immensity of the undertaking became apparent. Similarly, the Irish systems of government, politics and law superficially resembled their English counterparts. But in fact the very different contexts forced the apparently similar apparatus to work in totally different ways. Again, this became clearer in time, when the 'age of reform' began to alter the structure and spirit of English government. The same changes could not be carried out in Ireland without destroying the entire basis of the ascendancy, and imperilling the British domination. For this reason, among others, the role of the state in Ireland diverged increasingly from its role in Britain. At least, such was the initial outcome. In the longer term, the Irish experience began to feed back to the English systems, and to modify them materially. Nineteenth-century Ireland, W. L. Burn observes, formed 'a social laboratory. . . . The most conventional of Englishmen were willing to experiment in Ireland on lines which they were not prepared to contemplate or tolerate at home.'[1] The 'experiments' were initiated in no scientific or even rational spirit; 'expedients' would be an apter word. But, whatever they are called, important novelties and extraordinary devices were developed in Ireland; and, sooner or later, most of them were contemplated and even tolerated 'at home'.

The core of English local government in 1800 was the parish and the justice of the peace. But in Ireland the basic unit was the county, and the basic administrative instrument the county grand jury. This simple contrast in itself reveals two fundamental differences between the Irish and the English situations: first, that the Irish ruling class were much too few and scattered to govern individually or in twos and threes after the English fashion; and, secondly, that Ireland was much too poor for so small a unit as the parish to be administratively self-sufficient. In short, Ireland lacked the men and the material which made amateur government endurable in Britain. The administrative reforms of the first half, or even the first two-thirds, of the nineteenth century left the powers and position of the English JPs and parishes largely intact. They lost comparatively few functions to the central government; in fact, many new functions were thrust upon them initially. Elsewhere, they were often left to coexist with the new arms and agents of Whitehall. In Ireland, it was otherwise. Between 1815 and 1840, the Irish local authorities lost the bulk of their powers. The chief county officers were now appointed, and their salaries and duties fixed, by the central government. The undertaking of public works and the expenditure of public money in the localities were restricted by statute, and ultimately supervised and controlled from the centre. Moreover, inspectorates on a national basis were soon introduced. Even the earliest Irish county surveyors and prison inspectors were nationally appointed and conceived. Thus, whereas the first stage of administrative reform in English local government represented an attempt to broaden the relevant electorates, break the

Anglican monopoly of power and recruit JPs from outside the ranks of the traditional gentry, the equivalent phase in Ireland was marked by the passage of some of the old and almost all of the new functions of government from local to central control.

A similar divergence was apparent in urban government. The object of the English Municipal Reform Act of 1835 was to 'purify' and cheapen the working of the corporations and to extend the municipal franchise. In Ireland, on the other hand, most of the corporations were simply swept away. Even the ten left in being had a much more restricted franchise than did their English counterparts; and the central government was empowered to appoint some of their officers directly and to veto any of their bylaws at will. Otherwise, Irish urban government was directed from Dublin Castle in an authoritarian fashion scarcely imaginable in early Victorian White-hall, whence the new bureaucracy in England sallied, generally in vain, to overcome local resistance to positive innovation.

Public order followed the same course as local government. Whereas Britain has never achieved a national police force, and did not even possess county forces everywhere before the 1850s, Ireland began the nineteenth century with baronial forces and rapidly built up a national body to keep order and execute state policy uniformly throughout the island. By 1825 a single force for the entire country was well on the way to being realised. In 1822 the lord lieutenant was empowered to dismiss, equip and transfer members of the Irish police, all of whom were also to be subjected to the same inspectorate, discipline and regulations. A further refinement was the formation of a supernumerary mobile corps (about one thousand strong), the Peace Preservation Force, to be used in the 'disturbed districts', wherever these might be. Finally, the Irish police were brought under united command in 1836, with an autonomous, hierarchical in-spectorate to enforce, as the original recommendation put it, 'one uniform system of rules and regulations for the entire Irish police establishment'. The force was now fully national in scope and central in organisation. Specialisation and professionalism were also implicit and a single, large training depot in Dublin was set up to serve the whole body. Thus Ireland possessed a coherent, stratified, para-military police at a time when the lonely, untrained village constable was still the instrument of law enforcement over most of rural England. Local justice matched public order. Whereas in England, the amateur, unpaid JP continued to deal with petty crime and lesser civil matters – in fact, continues to do so to some extent even to the present day – an opposite system developed gradually in Ireland. Paid and often professional magistrates, resident in their particular localities, came to engross the first judicial level throughout the country. Again, the trend towards a specialised and authoritarian service contrasted strikingly with the English experience.

Why, in all these areas of day-to-day government, did Ireland move in a different direction from her master? One reason is, as we have suggested, that Ireland lacked the basis for effective amateur administration. So long as it was accepted that local government might be the monopoly of a clique, however small, inefficient or corrupt, this scarcely mattered. But when the wind of change began to blow, England possessed the human and economic resources to renew, to some extent, the old system upon broader and more active principles, but Ireland did not. Any step to democratise Irish local government would have admitted Catholics to a share in power, and introduced factional struggles in the representative institutions. Faced with this possibility, Irish Protestants acquiesced in centralisation, which offered better security for their material interests, in much the same fashion as they had preferred the Act of Union to the dangers of active Catholic participation in a domestic political system. Moreover, all the English arrangements rested upon a certain measure of public spirit among the gentry, and a certain correspondence of aims and sentiments between the JP and his charges. Of course, 'public spirit' was often but love of privilege, and there were always fundamental divergences of interest between proprietor, farmer and tenant – sometimes the parson, too, might be included. But even at its worst this was still a far cry from the naked rapacity, irresponsibility and savagery which characterised Irish rural relations in most areas. Many exceptions can be named, but in general Irish landlords and agents behaved and were treated as if they were at war with their dependents. The English system made obeisance at least to the squirearchical tradition of duty and service. For the most part, the Irish gentry felt no greater sense of obligation to their tenants than did the Boer to the Kaffir; and they eschewed, instead of battling for, unrewarded labour for the state. Of course, the Union itself, representing as it did a failure of nerve on the part of the governing interests, tended to engender an *après moi le déluge* stance. It should also be remembered that the resident Irish ascendancy was impoverished and probably inferior in education and talent to its English counterpart. This last was both a function of size and a consequence of the high attractions of British or colonial careers for able men without openings at home. An even stronger contrast might be made between the mercantile and manufacturing classes in the two countries. As to the police and judicial forces, British opinion needed no persuasion that Ireland required a more rational, elaborate and autocratic system of repression than was the case with happier lands.

The field of social welfare in part resembles, and in part differs from, that of public order and local government. In certain aspects of social welfare, the characteristics which we have described above were repeated. But in at least one other – and that the most important of all – an English model was imposed on Ireland, and an attempt made to render the systems in the two countries identical. In public health (to take an example of the first type), Ireland was *formally* more advanced than Britain during most of the nineteenth century. As early as 1805 provision was made for Irish public dispensaries, half of the cost of which was met from public funds. In theory, the dispensaries furnished free medicine and free medical attention to the poor. They spread rapidly, if haphazardly; by 1840 over six hundred had been established. The quality and effectiveness of this facility were probably very bad. But at least an organisation and a principle had been established; England was to lack both for several decades still to come. Moreover, every county inherited from the eighteenth century at least one infirmary and one fever hospital maintained from the local rates; and from early in the nineteenth century all appointments to these seventy-four institutions were made by public authorities. Even the so-called private hospitals were semi-state establishments in Ireland, being supported by initial or recurrent grants from the central government.

The Irish treatment of insanity was marked by two very interesting developments in the first quarter of the nineteenth century. One was the grouping together of adjacent counties for the establishment of large regional mental hospitals, ten in all. The other was a centralised, national system of control and inspection to secure uniformity. Once again, the contrast with English heterogeneity, localism and *laissez-faire* is most arresting. If one takes policy and structure as the criteria, Ireland had one of the most advanced health services in Europe in the first half of the nineteenth century. It was to a large degree state-supported, uniform and centralised. It aimed at providing the poor – that is, the huge bulk of the population – with some security against both minor and major illness, and at rationalising and specialising the hospital services. For example, twenty-one of the thirty Dublin hospitals in 1840 specialised in one branch of medicine or another. It is, of course, impossible to gauge the efficiency of this system, especially at so early a stage of modern medical science; and, however efficacious, it cannot possibly have sufficed to meet the needs of poverty in what was mainly a subsistence economy. None the less, the very mechanics of the system and the ideas which it embodied were remarkably sophisticated. It cannot have been altogether a coincidence that the years 1830–50 constituted a Golden Age of Irish medicine and medical discovery and research.

In contrast to this field of social welfare, in which Ireland moved swiftly toward modern forms while Britain was relatively immobile, the English Poor Law, 'invented' in 1834, was simply translated across St George's Channel four years later. The English Poor Law was ill designed even for England. It attempted to combine security against actual starvation with a compulsion upon the working class to enter the 'free labour market'. The instrument of both the security and the compulsion was the grim, residential workhouse, where life was to be 'less eligible' than that of the lowest paid wage-earner. It was inappropriate even for England in that the poor who could not work – infants, the old and the sick – were equally condemned to the 'less eligible' existence, and also in that it failed to provide at all for the short-term heavy unemployment which characterised the industrial economy in the early phase of alternating boom and slump. But whatever its relevance to England, 'to force labour into the open market' was meaningless in Ireland, where no demand whatever was matched by a practically limitless supply. Similarly, to compel the able-bodied Irish poor to enter workhouses was also to compel them to throw up their land and with it all hopes of re-entering their own economy. No alternative holding or employment was ever likely to be available. The more general prospect was as follows: either the great majority of the Irish peasants would still continue to cling to their land, in which case the problem of Irish poverty would remain untouched; or else a large number of them would break under some sudden strain – as was indeed to happen in the famine – in which case neither the workhouses nor the rates could bear the burden. In short, the English type of Poor Law could neither ward off the impending disaster in Ireland nor cope with its effects when it arrived.

The Poor Law is, then, a great exception to the rule that Irish government deviated increasingly from English until the close of the nineteenth century. The probable reasons for this exception are interesting. Unlike England, Ireland had no Poor Law before 1834, and when one was first proposed in 1833 a special Irish Poor Inquiry Commission was established. The majority of the Commission fairly rejected the new English model as either irrelevant or damaging in Irish circumstances. Instead, they proposed reducing the pressure on the soil by mass emigration, and by increasing employment through reclaiming waste lands and fostering indigenous industry such as fishing; their main hopes, however, were pinned on the first resource, emigration. Why did the British government reject these recommendations? Probably because mass emigration would have been hugely expensive – up to £20 million for several years – if the scale were to be large enough to achieve the object; because Westminster would have been called on to share the financial and administrative load; and because the Irish landowners would have been subjected to a compulsory levy, while Irish pauperism would have become a national rather than a local liability.

In contrast, the English model, which the government now proceeded to foist on Ireland, was supposed to be the cheapest possible, and it threw the entire burden upon the particular Irish localities concerned. The Commission's scheme would have offended four important assumptions of the British elite: that the state should spend as little money as was practicable; that the economic interests of landed proprietors should be cherished; that Britain should not support Irish parasites; and that poverty was entirely a local responsibility. The transference of the 1834 Poor Law to Ireland minimised the encroachments upon these principles. Herein lies the probable explanation of the eccentric course followed in this branch of economic and social reform. In fact, even in this case, the Irish pressures wrought some changes. On the one hand, the centralised and professional nature of Irish government ensured that the establishment of workhouses there was achieved with a speed and ease quite unlike the painful, patchy and contested English undertakings. On the other hand, the Irish Poor Law was soon penetrating – because of the sheer necessities of the case – into areas far removed from the original scheme, such as pharmacy and technical education.

Irish poverty also bred state activity of a more positive kind. One form was the continuation and embellishment of the eighteenth-century Irish tradition of government support for public works. This was, of course, more than a tradition; it was a near necessity where famine was never far away and the economy pitifully undeveloped. One of the most striking innovations of the early nineteenth century was the establishment in 1817 of a central loan fund for Irish public works, as a charge upon the imperial revenue. The advances from this fund were not confined to public buildings, roads and bridges; fisheries, mines and even communal resettlement projects were beneficiaries. The door was opening into a crude species of economic planning. In 1831 the Board of Works, with a national inspectorate of engineers, was re-established as a substantially new department. The Board spent over £1 million during the next eight years, by outright grants as well as loans. The inspectorate, as was commonly the case, tended to produce uniformity and coherence in administration, and to initiate a cycle of governmental growth. Centralisation and the needs of supervision led to some degree of planning, if only to establish priorities in expenditure. In time, the corps developed its own expertise, and the largeness of their tasks led them into distant fields: for example, they had virtually to determine the wage rates in areas – and there were many of these – where there was little cash employment outside the public works. This in turn forced them into the realm of wage policy and even economic theorising.

The Great Famine brought a sudden multiplication of the Board's activities as public works were hastily enlarged (and invented) to provide cash income. This expansion was short-lived as well as chaotic; but despite the sedulous hostility of the 'reformed' treasury after 1850 to further state expenditure, the Board continued to accumulate new fields of action. By the last quarter of the nineteenth century it possessed a vast agglomeration of duties relating to both economic development and official and quasi-official construction. Its business embraced not merely public works and public building, but also loans for (and often the direct supervision of) land improvement, drainage, sanitation, dwellings for workers, parsons, priests, and teachers, piers and harbours, rail and tramway construction and many other matters. Of course, the quality of the administration and planning was poor. The Board's work was heaped up in an unthinking higgledy-piggledy fashion, while the treasury, obsessed with candle-ends, failed altogether to comprehend the needs and nature of Irish poverty. But whatever the manner and spirit of the state's intervention, the fact remained that the state had had to intervene – to prime, regulate and underpin the economy to an extent which would have been unthinkable in contemporary England.

Education manifested a second type of extraordinary state action which derived from Irish poverty. The British government would not stand by and see an independent Catholic system develop – if indeed such a development were possible at all. It might teach 'sedition' and 'superstition'. It would certainly be intrinsically bad, deficient in both capital and revenue, and very slow to grow. Yet there was an equal fear – sharpened by Malthus and memories of the French Revolution – of the economic and political dangers of illiteracy. The way out of this dilemma chosen by the new Whig-Liberal government in 1831 was one in which the state predominantly, though not exclusively, undertook a gigantic scheme of elementary schooling. Two-thirds of the costs of buildings and equipment, and of salaries and other running expenses, were provided out of public funds.

This state aid carried with it state control over much of the syllabus and teaching. The new Board of Education possessed a veto over appointments, laid down teaching methods and prescribed the books for class use. These powers were real from the outset because an inspectorate to report on the schools and to set and maintain standards had been established simultaneously with the Board. Moreover, teacher training was part of the original plan. 'Model schools' were soon set up, and thenceforth only teachers qualified therein might be employed in the state system. By 1840 several training colleges were in operation, and the entire country had been divided into inspectoral districts – roughly one per county. In short, a uniform, co-ordinated, and national scheme of elementary education was under way. The next stage was the gradation and promotion of teachers, and the fixing of their salaries, by the Board. Not only did state intervention in education intensify rapidly; it also spread horizontally. Vocational education began with a dozen agricultural schools. Secondary education, though still substantially independent, was subjected to some degree of central inspection (and therefore standardisation), especially after the Board began to dispense grants and determine examinations.

Peel's 'Godless colleges' of 1845 – the first of innumerable failures to solve the problem of Irish university education – showed the limits of state action in this area. The state could only work effectively, so far as the mass of the Irish population was concerned, in conjunction with another power, the Catholic Church. Generally speaking, the farther on in the century and the higher up on the educational scale, the more difficult it was for the two bodies to reach a *modus vivendi*. The elementary school system, which embraced the great majority of Irish children within twenty years of its institution, would scarcely have succeeded had it been launched in 1861 instead of 1831, or had it extended to subjects with more philosophical or theological content than the three Rs. Yet this is merely to say that the antagonistic positions of both church and state hardened as the nineteenth century progressed, and that state education in Ireland was never a fully secular system, but rather a secular-clerical hybrid. It is not to suggest that at any level, least of all the lowest, the Irish educational system could have been developed without the state. For all their crudeness, the elementary schools were perhaps the greatest single benefit of the British connection in the middle decades of the nineteenth century. Certainly they were a benefit which many contemporary English children of equivalent status did not enjoy. Perhaps no country with nearly so low a per capita income as Ireland had nearly so high a literacy rate in the second half of the nineteenth century; and this despite the absence of compulsion to attend and the irregularity of attendance of many older children.

The four cases of order, welfare, planning and education suffice to indicate the very different types of state which developed in the United Kingdom after the Act of Union. In contrast to the British, Irish government was remarkable for the extent to which centralisation, uniformity, inspection and professionalism spread throughout the system before 1850. It would be wrong to assume automatically that the similar trends in British government, especially in the late

Victorian and Edwardian periods, derived simply and directly from the Irish experience. The feeling that Ireland was *sui generis* was universal. This cut both ways. It enabled some English intellectuals to press for revolutionary changes in Ireland which were altogether incompatible with received doctrine in Great Britain. But a more general effect was to engender the comfortable illusion that what happened in Ireland had no necessary repercussions beyond the island's shores. Moreover, contemporaries were very ill informed about both the operations of executive government and Irish circumstances; it is difficult to think of any two subjects of comparable importance about which nineteenth-century Englishmen entertained so many and such facile misconceptions. Thirdly, we must recollect that, with the exception of the Poor Law, all the developments in government which we have mentioned were *ad hoc* responses to specific pressures and emergencies, not segments of a total plan or derivatives of a general theory. Growing quietly and naturally in the Irish environment, most of the measures attracted little attention, and where justification was attempted, it was in terms of expediency or immediate necessity. The common elements in the state intervention in the various Irish fields, and the sort of state which they logically implied and were gradually realising, were only revealed in retrospect.

All this is but a caution against rash *post hoc propter hoc* assumptions. When all the necessary allowances and qualifications have been made, the over-riding fact remains that Britain and Ireland constituted a single kingdom with the same law-making agency and a common pool of political and professional administrators at the highest level. The force of example and precedent constantly worked below the surface; and even overhead, the Irish apprenticeship of so many British statesmen, from Peel and Stanley at one end of the century to Randolph Churchill and Balfour at the other, enlarged the administrative horizons of the homeland. More important still, if even more difficult to quantify, was the slow corrosion of a basic presupposition of mid-Victorian Britain: that she herself represented a norm in government and economic organisation to which other advanced states would gradually approximate. Over time, the Irish experience revealed to British opinion how exceptional, curious and accidental so many of the systems obtaining in Great Britain really were. In part, the process was one of self-revelation. Dr Stokes's observation about another dependency is equally pertinent to Ireland: 'British rule in India was not a disconnected fragment of English history but even from the most insular standpoint it holds a mirror up to nature, reflecting the English mind and character in a way that often escapes the Englishman confined in his domestic setting.'[2] Ireland showed in macrocosm some of the forces making for collectivism everywhere. Slowly it became apparent that, however vast the differences between the two countries, many were differences of degree rather than of kind; and that so far from bringing Ireland painfully to the stage at which *laissez-faire* might be safely loosed, the Irish trend merely anticipated, not to say abetted, a similar trend in Britain. The pressures were stronger in the weaker island, but they worked in both.

It is true that not only was Ireland desperately poor, but also that she could not accumulate capital or attract investment from private sources to a significant degree. It is true that the condition of most of her inhabitants was more than pathetic – it was 'intolerable' when advertised; and that she advertised the evils violently and incessantly, in Westminster, in Boston and, most effectively, in her own country-side. It is true that British assumptions about Ireland militated against active local government there, and tended to promote olympianism, specialisation and arbitrariness among even the best of Irish administrators. At first sight, the contrast with Britain in all of these respects seems striking. But when we consider the matter more closely and separate the substance from the accidents, it becomes apparent that Ireland was merely exhibiting, in a particularly inter-connected and dramatic form, general features of mid- and late nineteenth-century government and life. Poverty was endemic in Britain, too; and however large they may have been, British capital and investment in the nineteenth century were not so distributed or deployed as to be likely to eradicate it. Social and occupational 'problems' abounded there as well; and sooner or later most were advertised, attracting in turn general regulatory legislation and central supervisory and enforcing bodies. For all the idiosyncrasies of Irish squalor and the depth of Irish helplessness, Ireland's needs differed in intensity and form of manifestation rather than in type from those of the other island. No departure in Ireland was ultimately irrelevant to Britain.

So far we have considered Ireland mainly as a drastic or active element in the governmental structure of the United Kingdom. But the survey would be incomplete without looking upon her in the opposite – the pathetic or passive – role as well. Here the obvious case for analysis is land and property. For the first two-thirds of the nineteenth century, Parliament dealt with the question of Irish land almost exclusively on the basis of British experience. In practice this meant that the land legislation from 1801 to 1870 was, in general, in the interest of the Irish landlord and against the interest of the Irish tenant. It is true that throughout this period Irish landlords directly, and through marriage networks, enjoyed a large influence in the leadership of both the Whig and Tory parties and in both Houses (but especially in the Lords) out of all proportion to their numbers. Naturally this influence coloured government measures. But the decisive factor was not so much class pressure exercised within cabinets and on front benches, as the dominant English ideas on landed property in the late Georgian and early and mid-Victorian periods.

In the first third of the nineteenth century, educated opinion generally assumed that ownership should be untrammelled legally by social obligations or other objectives. The good landlord would instinctively shoulder some responsibility for the well-being of the tenants, labourers and others in his territorial sphere. But defining this responsibility in statute and rendering it enforceable at law were no more to be thought of than, say, compelling business corporations to set up educational foundations would be today. It was a private matter: at the very most, one of conscience. In law, ownership was an absolute condition.

Such a philosophy was clearly reflected in the pre-Victorian legislation at Westminster. It would be wrong to suppose there was no, or very little, Irish land legislation before 1840; in fact, many Acts were passed. But these were Acts designed to secure the land-lord's position by cheapening and facilitating ejectments, evictions and the consolidation of holdings, and by attempting to render these courses physically safer through stamping out peasant counter-measures. Many of the contemporary political economists argued or implied – as doubtless their intellectual descendants would argue today – that this type of legislation was in Ireland's long-term interests, in driving the population off the land, preparing the way for raising livestock in their places and in general establishing a more viable economy. But the early nineteenth-century land legislation did not derive from the economists (although most of them endorsed it warmly), but from the fact that the conventional British notions of land ownership were transferred uncritically to Ireland upon the prompting of Irish proprietors or the provocation of Irish dis-turbances.

The next phase, roughly 1840 to 1870, bore rather the impress of Manchester radicalism. The first signs of change appeared in Peel's second administration, 1841–6. Peel himself had some knowledge of and little sympathy with Irish landlords whom he regarded as irresponsible as a class, grasping only the rights of property and ignoring its duties. He had begun to adumbrate in a rudimentary form the policy later to be known as 'killing Home Rule by kindness', and among his measures for outbidding O'Connell's repeal move-ment in the early 1840s he contemplated relief for the Irish smallholders, although, as things turned out, this bill was never carried. Again, Peel set up a royal commission in 1843 to inquire into Irish land tenures, and such an investigation was normally an overture to remedial legislation as well as an underminer of the status quo. Thus the first stirrings of agrarian reform can be discerned in 1843–5. Three features are especially noteworthy. For the first time the problem of Irish land was being considered primarily as a peasant's rather than as a proprietor's problem. Next, this happened, although the connection was as yet oblique, under political pressure from Ireland. Finally, a great body of reliable information had been collected on a subject hitherto widely canvassed but not really known. In short, the 1880s were foreshadowed.

The late 1840s witnessed further developments in the same direction. During the Great Famine, Irish landlordism was greatly discredited among the British public, who believed that they were being saddled with relief expenses which the proprietors should properly have borne. In consequence legislation was passed in 1847–9 to redress this supposed injustice, and to facilitate the transference of Irish land from the hands of financially embarrassed Irish landlords to more solvent owners. The Encumbered Estates Act of 1849, which embodied this last objective, has been aptly described as an attempt to establish a free trade in Irish land. Like the other Irish land legislation between 1845 and 1865, the Act was 'reformist' in the Manchester or Cobdenite sense of the term. It aimed at making landlord-tenant relations wholly a matter of 'free contract' (as against status and custom); at eliminating entail and primogeniture and similar clogs upon the purchase and sale of land; at enabling open competition and the unfettered pressures of supply and demand to establish the level of rents and the terms of tenancy agreements – in short, at making all aspects of land tenure subject to the play of capitalism and the market. Ironically enough, over precisely the same period, 1845–65, the Irish tenant demands crystallised at last into a specific programme, the objects of which were directly opposite to those of free trade radicalism. Two of the '3 Fs' into which the programme had been summarised, fixed tenure and fair rents, asked, respectively, for security of possession for the tenant and rent control, both to be enforced by the state upon the proprietor. Once again, then, in the mid- as well as the early Victorian years, British policy was proceeding from concepts of property and from analyses of Irish economic difficulties which were totally alien to Ireland.

As before, the official policy was endorsed by most orthodox political economists. 'Profits or perish' had become the simple universal, applicable to every economic situation; 'the forces of the market' constituted, collectively, the new god. But again the theorists did not directly influence the legislation, which was still primarily a reflection of the assumptions currently predominant among the educated classes of Great Britain, although of course the theorists had played some part in crystallising this opinion. Dr Black sums up the story admirably:

> . . . economic policy in Ireland may appear as a tangled, drab skein of shifts and expedients, but up to Gladstone's time there is a central thread running through it – the settlement of landlord-tenant relationships on a contract basis, and the creation of conditions suitable to farming on the English model. But it seems fair to say that legislators adopted this approach not so much because it embodied the advice of the economists, as because it accorded with the ideas and wishes of the landowning classes, then still dominant in both Houses of Parliament. It may appear strange that the proposals of the economists accorded so well with the interests of the landlords, when traditionally the economists have been depicted as the champions of the urban middle class against the old landed aristocracy; but it should be remembered that the economists' quarrel was not with the landlords as land-lords, but as protectionists.[3]

But if Ireland was passive, helplessly subjected to British concepts, for the first two-thirds of the nineteenth century, she ultimately won her ideological revenge, undermining English presuppositions upon property and destroying some important constituents of classical political economy.

Down to the Great Famine, the British political economists did not modify their basic theory when confronted by its patent in-applicability to Ireland. Instead, they demanded the modification of Irish circumstances so that their basic theory might apply. Concretely, this meant the removal of three-fifths of the rural population from the soil, and the consolidation of holdings after the English pattern. In this phase, the economists did not seriously consider what was to become of the 4 or 5 million uprooted persons; nor did they realise, let alone sympathise with, the Irish peasant's hostility to a rural economy of the English type. Yet by 1840 all the main elements present in the property revolution of 1870–1903 had struck the surface. These derived, not from the theoretical economists, but from Irish proprietors, land-agents and farmers, from William Conner, Sharman Crawford, William Blacker and J. F. Lalor. In 1830 Conner argued for fixing rents by arbitration instead of competition, and for absolute security of tenure subject to the payment of fixed rent. This was 'dual ownership' in embryo. From 1835 on, Crawford pressed for compensation for improvement. In 1836 Blacker set out the justification of the small holding on economic grounds, and looked to 'durable and certain interest' to provide the other Irish desiderata, social security and conditions favourable to capital accumulation and investment. Lalor associated social, economic and political revolution. It was these advocates, then, who provided the theoretical framework on which the Tenant League and its various successors were to rest. They also anticipated in all essentials the turnabout of the political economists in the late 1860s, and the remedial land legislation of the following generation.

In 1846–8, under the impact of the Great Famine and the writings of Blacker and similar Continental commentators, the *avant garde*, notably John Stuart Mill, began to question the universal applicability of political economy. But this was no real revolt. Mill as yet advocated little more than 'home colonisation', or the resettlement of the surplus peasantry upon waste lands, as a preliminary to establishing English capitalistic farming in the 'cleared regions'. Not until 1865 was there a fundamental deviation. In that year, J. E. Cairnes (who lived in Ireland) first argued for peasant proprietorship upon the ground that property in land was not absolute but qualified, and subject to the labourer's right to a share of the fruits of his work.

Thus at last the Irish demands for a radically different form of society, and the metaphysics underlying these demands, were being reflected by certain of the economists. Cairnes and Mill (in *England and Ireland*, 1868) were using much the same equipment as Ricardo and Torrens had done forty years before. But they had abandoned two vital presuppositions of the old political economy: first, that property rights were absolute, and second, that England formed either a norm or an ideal society. The final revolution was epitomised by the clash between Robert Lowe and Mill on 12 March 1868, in the House of Commons, in which Lowe fought in the traditional fashion for 'the principles of political economy' as ultimate and invariable, while Mill announced their relativity with, 'I am sure that no one is at all capable of determining what is the right political economy for any country until he knows its circumstances'. This was the climacteric. The onset of economic relativism, together with the actual demands – largely Irish – which hastened its emergence, mark one of the most important turning points in modern British history, no less than in the history of economic thought.

In legislative as distinct from intellectual terms, the turning point was Gladstone's first Land Act of 1870. Perhaps we should say a half-turning point. The measure was presented as quite orthodox – that is, as fully respecting the rights of property – and the best proof that it was accepted as such was the lack of serious opposition in either House of Parliament. This conviction was not immediately disturbed as the Act was practically inoperative. From the very beginning its principles, as set out by Gladstone, seemed comparatively harmless. These were to render statutory the 'Ulster custom' (the outgoing tenant's right to sell his 'interest') wherever that usage was in force in Ireland; in other places, to compensate the evicted tenant for disturbance according to a fixed scale of damages, unless the cause of the eviction was non-payment of rent; and to compensate the tenant for improvements in the property even if the cause of his eviction was non-payment of rent. The provisions of the Act gave the tenant little that he really wanted, still less perhaps of what he really needed. It concentrated upon rendering him more secure in his holding but without going nearly the length of the first of the '3 Fs', fixity of tenure. It also refused the second and most important 'F', fair rent, altogether. No reductions or even controls were proposed. In fact, landlords were still quite free in theory to raise rents to whatever level was necessary in order to eject their tenants on the ground of non-payment of rent, thereby escaping all obligation to compensate them for disturbance – although the tenants' psychological, political and other intimidatory weapons induced most of them to opt for a quiet life. Thus the tenant had some reason for supposing that the 1870 Act represented a mere tinkering with the existing system. But he would have been wrong to do so.

The right to compensation for improvements made without the landlord's consent, the limitation upon his powers to evict, and the statutory recognition that a tenant might own a saleable interest in his land, all denied the landlord unbridled control over his own property. The corollary was of course that this property was no longer wholly 'private'. The tenant now possessed legal rights, calculable in money terms, in the same soil, and the landlord could not deal with it as he wished. In short, in some rudimentary sense or other, joint proprietorship had been established. Perhaps it merely legalised the status quo. But mere legalisation in such a case is revolutionary. As A. V. Dicey noted, 'Law is in itself the creator of law-making opinion'. Because of the general ambivalence of the Act, and its weak drafting, the tenants' victory of 1870 was essentially moral or ideological rather than concrete. But the breakthrough in ideas was in the long run all-important. Moreover, Gladstone, the very pivot of mid-Victorian politics, the principal heir of both Cobdenite and Peelite political traditions, and the destined captain of reform for two decades still, had been moved to act, not by direct pressure, but by the conviction that he was correcting an original and historic injustice. This meant that whatever was said in Parliament at its introduction, the 1870 Act was not a final settlement but the start of a new process of amelioration, once time had shown that the Act had altered nothing. It also heralded a dynamic and self-consciously experimental approach to Irish social problems, one of the fruits of which was, of course, Gladstone's own conversion to Home Rule.

The dialectical but empty triumph of 1870 was translated into substantial achievement for the tenants under the pressure of agricultural distress in the late 1870s and mid-1880s, when farm prices and incomes fell catastrophically. The inability of the tenants to pay rents at the old levels led, not to reductions in their obligations, but to evictions upon a scale unknown since the 1840s. The corollary was renewed tenant militancy and the reorganisation of their forces, political and terroristic. The familiar pattern of coercion-cum-concession was to be repeated over and over again. The first critical concession was Gladstone's second Land Act in 1881. This fully adopted the '3 Fs' which had constituted the tenants' official programme for more than a generation – that is to say, it provided for free sale as well as fixity of tenure and fair rents. The Land Act of 1881 was thus an undisguised acceptance of co-ownership, with the state permanently involved in the conflict between the wrangling partners through the institution of land courts empowered to fix rents. The continuation of tenant 'warfare' meant that the Act itself led to further concessions. In fixing rents the new land courts were influenced (a euphemism perhaps for intimidated) by the sustained agrarian agitation, while in 1882 the government further surrendered by using public monies to wipe off the rent arrears of some of the tenants who could not take advantage of the new courts while their obligations to the landlords were outstanding. As Sir Michael Hicks-Beach had observed when Irish secretary a little time before, 'If there is one thing which strikes Englishmen who have to deal with Irish matters, more than another, it is that, whereas in England we have something like a dread of government interference, in Ireland that interference, if not actually courted, seems at any rate to be expected'.

This second wave of reform was, then, notable for two departures. The first was the attempt to solve the problem by conceding more and more to the tenant programme; the second, to make that programme practicable by allowing for the changes in farm income and in the tenant's capacity to pay which the agricultural depression had brought about. But even this was still the old story of too little too late. With agricultural prices continuing to fall and tenant expectations continuing to rise, the lag between the remedy applied and the farmer's needs remained throughout the rest of the nineteenth century. By the time that the tenant programme of the '3 Fs' had been adopted, it no longer satisfied the smallholders. At least here, the threadbare joke, that the trouble with the Irish Question was not that the English could not find an answer but that the Irish kept changing the Question, had point. By the 1880s the real demand was not dual ownership but peasant proprietorship. A token concession in this direction had been made as early as 1870, at John Bright's instigation; but like the other elements in Gladstone's first Act, the scheme of state loans to assist individual tenants to buy out their holdings was practically ineffective. It was the Conservative 'Caretakers' administration of 1885 – temporarily in a tacit alliance with the Irish Party – which took the first significant step toward state assistance for land purchase, although its measure was so narrowly framed as to be useful only to the most prosperous tenants – those who least needed aid.

A stream of other Bills and statutes followed in the last fifteen years of the nineteenth century. These all continued, and from the tenants' point of view improved upon, the lines of legislation already laid down – that is, confirming and extending the tenant's share in dual ownership; writing off arrears; enabling or inducing the land courts to fix lower rents, and to refix them at shorter intervals; and easing the conditions of land purchase. The only new feature was Balfour's policy of special treatment for the most depressed areas, inaugurated by the institution of the congested district boards in 1891. This involved the state – at least indirectly – in promoting employment, establishing minor industry and light railways, clearing poor land and removing population from the worst-stricken regions of the south and west. The next and last really revolutionary change was the Land Act of 1903. This was revolutionary in that it was based – apparently – upon consent, upon agreements freely entered into by landlords and tenants. If this were all, it would of course have failed. But three further provisions of the Act made a large scale change in the ownership of land practicable at last. First, it dealt with entire estates instead of individual holdings; secondly, it provided massive state grants to induce both parties to come to settlements (about one-eighth of the purchase price being provided directly from government funds); and, thirdly, it offered tenants loans for purchases upon such cheap and favourable terms that practically all could accept. Largely because of traditional suspicions and the political exploitation of these suspicions on both sides, as noted above, the 1903 Act did not immediately achieve the universal transference in land ownership which it proposed. But in the long run, supplemented by further concessions, it issued in the general social revolution whereby rural Ireland became a nation of petty freeholders.

The 1903 Act was not a socialist measure insofar as such alternatives as the nationalisation of land or collective farming were rejected. It was even possible, if not very plausible, for its Conservative supporters to argue that the state was merely stepping in to set the social organisation upon a new basis; that once this was accomplished it could retire; in short, that the interference was not 'permanent'. The truth was, however, that a social and economic transformation of the first magnitude, of the same order as that begun in France in 1789, had been initiated. A once-ruling class was to be dispossessed, even if most tenderly and on favourable terms. 'Dispossession' is scarcely too strong a term, because the alternative of compulsory purchase of estates had been long in the wings and would certainly have taken the stage if all the proprietors had proved intransigent. Moreover, to achieve this tremendous turnabout, the government had used subsidies upon a scale unknown since the abolition of slavery in 1833.

This use of state power, financial and indirectly coercive, marked a final break with the Victorian concepts of public responsibility and private right. As to the area of land involved, one would have to look back to the original Irish plantations, or to the distribution of monastic lands in England in the sixteenth century, for parallels. Most important of all, the conception of society as operating on an essentially individualist and contractual basis, in which market forces were the proper determinant of social and economic good, had been irremediably breached. The great example of Ireland passive under British rule became in the end a paradigm of Ireland drastic.

> The man that once did sell the Lion's skin
> While the beast liv'd, was killed with hunting him.

The subjects considered in this chapter are a mere selection. A multitude of other Irish innovations, from the development of the 'intermediate prison' system to cereal research, from the control of the salmon fishing industry to the treatment of tuberculosis as a question of public health, could have been called in to embroider the theme of regional ferment sooner or later affecting the entire United Kingdom. Correspondingly, the Irish use of dominion status after 1921 to emasculate the empire whose interests it was meant to secure is one of many political counterparts to the changes in economic theory and the *étatisme* which the Irish land question helped to release. But the points have been made. What finally needs stressing is perhaps the obverse side of these developments. For it is also true that the complete structure and genius of Irish government after independence was British – or at the very least, British as honed and tempered by Irish responsibilities. The training and ideal of the public official, his hierarchical organisation, his relationships to politics, the conventions governing his conduct – all bear the impress of Whitehall. Since her new administrative system was one of the foremost creations of Great Britain in her century of greatest creativity, the new state was generally regarded as fortunate in this retention. The conclusion is none the less ironic. Each of the Siamese twins – hateful to one another joined, resentful severed – could not but see, if he looked honestly, his own features in the other's face.

3
Disaffection

Militant, doctrinaire nationalism declined immediately after the Act of Union. Robert Emmet's Dublin Rebellion of 1803 was a sordid fiasco, even if it subsequently added to the rhetoric and hagiography of the Republicans. The critical happenings of the first half of the nineteenth century belong to another sphere. The failure to grant Catholic Emancipation, and the attempts (1808–15) of the British government to intervene in the elections of the Irish Catholic bishops, prepared the church for participation in parliamentary politics. This was to have momentous consequences. The early nineteenth-century British policies also destroyed the governmental strategy of taming the Catholic masses through influencing the priests, the only extensive literate Catholic group and in many ways the natural and inevitable leaders of their congregations. The church had unmatched resources of organisation and management in Ireland; once these were thrown into battle, it emerged, not only victorious on the issue which had roused it to action, but also politically conscious and effective. The church-in-politics was one of the main determinants of nineteenth-century Irish history, even if it also engendered many embarrassments and tensions in both the religious and the nationalist camps.

The prime architect of the new order was Daniel O'Connell. Working increasingly with and through the church, he built up the native political power from 1808 to the formation of the Catholic Association in 1823. In 1826–8 the Association struck decisively by defeating landlord-supported candidates at by-elections. Clerical support and clerical deployment of the tenant vote had forged a weapon which could win one-third of the constituencies of Ireland, evictions and other punishments notwithstanding. It was this demonstration of strength which broke the Tory resistance to emancipation. 'All the great interests broke down and the desertion has been universal', the defeated candidate reported to Peel from the scene of battle in Clare in July 1828. 'Such a scene as we have had! Such a tremendous prospect as opens before us.' Of 'that fevered exhibition of sobered and desperate enthusiasm', Peel himself asked, 'Is it consistent with common prudence and common sense to repeat such scenes and to incur such risks of contagion?'

It is noteworthy that the government's original emancipation proposals included three counter-measures: the proscription of political organisations like the Association, the disfranchisement of the forty-shilling freeholders and the payment of the Catholic clergy by the state. Each was designed to remove a major part of the new political machine, for, indeed, nothing less than a political machine was what they had to deal with, O'Connell having laid the foundations of an Irish parliamentary party, not to say the foundations of the first parliamentary party of the modern era. The Association was centrally organised. It approved the candidates. The candidates whom it approved for selected constituencies were certain of election. If they broke their pledges to the Association they were certain of defeat upon the next occasion. The Association drew a large annual income (up to £300,000 perhaps in present values), for political purposes, from the network of parishes through the 'penny rent'. The clergy acted as local and constituency organisers, passed down directives, and above all gathered, led and steadied the voters on the day of polling.

Down to 1840 O'Connell used this instrument, and the little body of committed followers which it gave him in the House of Commons, to considerable effect. He deployed the power which derived from obedient votes – advertising its magnitude and suggesting the latent threat of revolution by means of the mass meeting – to secure specific legislative concessions and influence over the filling of Irish offices. Catholic emancipation itself was the firstfruit of this electoral power. From 1831 onwards O'Connell could bargain, to a limited extent, with the Whig-Liberals. The Lichfield House compact of 1835, whereby he promised support for a new Whig-Liberal ministry, secured a number of important legislative reforms, and a number of more congenial public appointments. It is significant that the main gains in the 1830s were in the field of religious equality. National education and the tithe commutation, municipal reform and civil marriages acts all tended to reduce the Protestant domination. O'Connell could still rely (although to a much lesser extent) upon church power to underpin the political system which had developed in several of the Irish constituencies. There was no longer a specific crusade like the movement for Catholic emancipation. But in many things the spiritual and political arms could still make common cause; and in the next decade, O'Connell was to prove himself capable of re-enlisting the church, virtually *en bloc*, in an agitation which was wholly radical and political in its stated object.

The O'Connellite strategy, however, could only operate under favourable conditions. In particular, it was only meaningful in fields and issues in which there was a considerable body of sympathy for the Irish objectives among the British members of Parliament and party leaders. O'Connell denied himself the additional resource of working with, or threatening to loose, the forces of physical violence. 'The winning of my country's freedom is not worth the shedding of a single drop of human blood' may have been the most courageous utterance ever made by a demagogue. But it also revealed a paucity of weapons. When, at last, O'Connell was forced to make repeal of the Union the foremost objective of his party, he was launched upon a campaign in which he could hope for no significant support in the House of Commons. To demonstrate outside the walls of the parliamentary system by mass rallies was a futile tactic if the government was prepared – as Peel's government was prepared – to use its forces to suppress assemblies. Peel could – and did – count upon O'Connell's pacifism. When, faced with the prospect of bloodshed, O'Connell called off the proscribed Clontarf meeting in 1843, it was a confession of political bankruptcy.

O'Connell's movement suffered from personal as well as institutional defects. He was himself a landlord, and most of his parliamentary supporters were landlords. Though by no means illiberal by contemporary standards, he was a poor conductor for the economic passions pent up in Ireland. Moreover, his 'progressivism' consisted partly in an inclination to be on the side of the philosophical radicals and free traders – even on such an issue as the repeal of the corn laws. This early Victorian radicalism had little relevance, was indeed an absolute hindrance to Irish social and agrarian reform as later generations understood the terms. Finally, O'Connell sought the political aggrandisement of his family, after the fashion of the old regime. He shared the fate of many another king in failing to provide successors of nearly his own capacity. For all these reasons, even if his political structure had gone unchallenged, it would almost certainly have collapsed upon his death. Yet, quite apart from his remarkable successes, his designs were of lasting significance. He set out, albeit in a rudimentary form, the basic patterns and strategy for the Irish parliamentary parties of the future. He harnessed, in general effectively, the powers of ecclesiastical organisation and of an aggrieved electorate. He inculcated in the masses of his country political awareness and expertise to a degree perhaps unparalleled in the Europe of his day. By the end, he had made himself, as Lamartine told him when he passed through Paris on his final journey, 'not only a man of one nation, you are a man of all Christendom'.

Thirty years of political confusion in Ireland followed O'Connell's death in 1847. Even had his son and political heir, John, been either able or trusted, he could not have kept the old group together. What coherence remained after 1843 was a tribute to his father's past achievements; by 1850 even the O'Connellites admitted that repeal was a dead issue. Yet a new, even a more powerful, Irish party might have developed in the 1850s. The Irish Reform Act of 1850 trebled the rural electorate, thereby increasing the number of 'popular' constituencies. Moreover, as we have seen, the repeal agitation of the early 1840s had brought the church back fully into politics. It is not easy to say why this happened. Of course, the clergy shared the impulses, as they shared the background, of their congregations; and they may have feared both a drift toward revolution, and alienation from their people, if they held aloof. At any rate, both the higher and the lower clergy publicly blessed and promoted O'Connell's last campaign. Thus with more 'open' constituencies and more clerical involvement a new advance seemed possible. Had it come, Westminster in the 1850s might have proved a good market: compacted votes commanded a high price in the unstable parliaments of the decade.

Yet no new Irish party materialised. No leader or programme nearly as dominant as O'Connell or repeal emerged; and, though in some respects the clergy filled the vacuum, they filled it with conflict rather than cohesion. During the early 1850s various fundamental divisions in political purpose, partly concealed before, came to the surface. Should the Irish party be completely independent of the Liberals, and act as a permanent opposition in the Commons? Or should it sell its support, selectively, for pieces of ameliorative legislation and posts of power and honour? Should it be a non-sectarian group, basing itself on radical and economic objects common to Irish Catholics and Presbyterians? Or should it act as Defender of the Faith, frankly recognising its Catholic base, and the enduring anti-Romanism in British and Ulster opinion? Should the priority be agrarian, educational, ecclesiastical or constitutional? Because these issues were never resolved, the Irish members broke eventually into tiny warring groups of irreconcilables, and by the end of the 1850s were as much attached to either the Liberals or the Conservatives as was the average English MP.

Part of the explanation of this failure to re-create an effective Irish party lies in the state of Irish society and the Irish economy after the Great Famine. The loss of some 3 million in population through death and emigration between 1845 and 1860 left Ireland temporarily inert. At the same time, 1851 ushered in a decade of gradual economic improvement, although the gains were much exaggerated by Englishmen. But the average size of holdings had increased dramatically in 1846–8; agricultural productivity rose; railways began to link most of rural Ireland to the ports and ultimately to growing British urban markets; in short, Ireland was enjoying – at a very considerable distance – the relatively full employment and rising real wages which characterised Great Britain in the 1850s. The combination of moral exhaustion, social dislocation and a dulling of the edge of poverty induced political sterility. Again, Ireland was, as ever, influenced by the British patterns. The very fact that 'party' was being damned and apparently expiring at Westminster coloured the outlook and affected the conduct of the Irish members. Personality also counted. The potential leaders of an Independent Irish Party, Frederick Lucas, Gavan Duffy, and G. H. Moore, were all personally unsuitable, lacking the passion or perseverance to dominate, and politically unlucky.

Intertwined with, and contributing to, their failures was Cardinal Cullen's first foray in politics. Cullen wished the Irish members to act as a Catholic lobby – which alienated Presbyterians, Anglicans, and many Catholic nationalists – and also to become a Liberal satellite, in order to secure influence with government. Thus, he worked against both political and confessional independence, and having lived long and risen high in Rome, his power over the Irish clergy (and indirectly over the Catholic population) was large. Cullen failed to manufacture the Irish party which he desired – his large power being both less than and different from that which he imagined – but he effectively destroyed all alternatives. He also engendered or deepened divisions in the ranks of the priests. The western province, under the influence of an anglophobe, Archbishop MacHale, largely repudiated his truckling to the Whigs and his attempts to influence legislation. Elsewhere, individual priests resisted Cullen publicly. The upshot was fraternal hate and Cullen's temporary withdrawal, followed by synodal decrees designed to produce a general clerical withdrawal, from Irish politics.

Beneath the surface, however, contrary forces were taking shape. O'Connell had blazed the trail at Westminster; he had begun the political enlightenment of the masses; he had involved the church in his movements. But in the end he had failed ingloriously; after 1843 his creations began to disintegrate until, two decades later, his purposes and techniques seemed almost to have vanished. The reactions to this depressing process included a revival of militancy and republicanism. The revival was gradual and marked by many turns of fortune. But three of its particular characteristics can be traced back to the initial Young Ireland deviation from O'Connell-ism. First was the nurturing – in some respects the invention – of a native culture. Its tone was one of total separation and self-assertion, perhaps more chauvinistic in the result than in the intention because of the inflation of its high-flown language and headlong romanticism. The growth of both literacy and effective communications between 1840 and 1855 gave its expression – first and foremost, the newspaper *Nation* – a currency and a purchase upon the popular imagination which would have been inconceivable in any earlier generation.

The second feature was the return of physical force to Irish nationalism after an absence of forty years. This was not premeditated. It was O'Connell's feud with the advanced young men, his deviousness and his final ineffectuality, which combined with parliamentary failure and famine at home to engender a feeling that violence was the only resort. The youth and rhetoric of the extremists, and their want of experience of bloodshed, must also be taken into account. Immediately the expression of this tendency was more than disastrous: it was tragicomic. The cruel subtitle of the 1848 rebellion, 'the battle of the Widow M'Cormick's cabbage plot', was scarcely unjustified. Ineptitude and plain bad luck placed the event in the same category as Feargus O'Connor's Chartist demonstration. In the long view, however, a new page in the book of revolution had been written. In the protracted trials and transportations which followed, some terrible beauty was born. Some heroism and dignity was manifested; more was imputed. Religious rancour was apparently overlaid: the northern Presbyterian, John Mitchel, and the southern Anglican, Smith O'Brien, were amongst the felons. Most important of all perhaps, some of the refugees, notably James Stephens, escaped to Paris, still the international school of serious revolution, where effective conspiracy and subversion might be learned. The ultimate consequence of this was the formation of the secret Irish Revolutionary (later Republican) Brotherhood in 1858.

Side by side with resort to violent means went the third development, a revival in the republican objective. Not merely did O'Connell's neo-Grattanism cease to appear a satisfactory goal. It was soon reasserted that an Irish Republic was more than a political aim, that beneath the appearances it was a fact. To the world at large the IRB (or Fenians) might appear a handful of self-appointed desperadoes, lacking electoral or any other popular sanction; but they saw themselves as the carriers of the national destiny. 'The Supreme Council . . .', the Constitution of the Brotherhood proclaimed, 'is hereby declared to be in fact, as well as by right, the sole Government of the Irish Republic. Its enactments shall be the Laws of the Irish Republic until Ireland secures absolute National Independence.' This was, essentially, the assertion which the United Irishmen had made. It was essentially the assertion which the 1916 revolutionaries and Dail Eireann in 1919–21 were to make. The claim might be demonstrated by a democratic majority; it did not depend upon it.

The IRB looked both backwards and forwards. It revived the old Jacobin doctrines of the United Irishmen: that the People was sovereign, and that the Party expressed its will and the Republic its political form. It repeated the cell organisation, the binding by oath and the conspiratorial mode. Conversely, 1916 has been justly described as an IRB rebellion, and Sinn Fein after 1917 was, in part, its creature and its heir. However, if Fenianism was rooted in Jacobinism, it developed new features to fit a new age. The most important was perhaps the use of North America, where nearly 3 million Irish now dwelt, as a base and source of money. But the attempts to provide regular military training and to recruit members among the Irish serving in the British army and Civil War veterans showed a practical strain hitherto absent from nineteenth-century Irish revolution, even if the wretched failures of Fenian 'operations' in Canada and Ireland during 1865–70 show that much amateurism survived.

Stephens, the original author of Fenian organisation, was a quarrelsome fanatic, but with the rise of younger men, in particular John Devoy, to influence in the IRB, the pragmatic, calculating element in the movement grew. When Devoy was released from prison and exiled to the United States in 1871, he concentrated his attention upon propaganda, the manipulation of American politics for Irish ends, and raising revenue, primarily for the purchase of arms. The para-revolutionary organisation which he and his supporters mainly used, Clan-na-Gael, was now designed to act as an auxiliary, behind the lines, to the Irish forces theoretically in the field. In fact, the opening of a systematic struggle for public opinion overseas, and the effective mobilisation of the Irish communities abroad, were radical innovations in the Anglo-Irish conflict. Devoy, therefore, carried considerable weight when he projected the 'New Departure' in 1879.

Exactly what the 'New Departure' signified may be disputed, but it certainly brought together for the first time the three great forces of modern Irish nationalism – the revolutionary, the civil and the parliamentary – and enabled them so to interact and supplement each other as to exert the maximum pressure upon the British government. At the head of the forces stood, respectively, Devoy, Michael Davitt and Charles Stewart Parnell. Their trust in one another and their co-operation were meagre and impermanent, but enough of a junction was made to render the early 1880s a period of signal Irish gains. When Devoy and other American Fenians 'newly departed' from the IRB's rigid rejection of parliamentary and other non-violent forms of agitation – 'it is time', Devoy said, 'we came out of the rat-holes of conspiracy' – they lent to Parnell and Davitt some of the magic of extremism, and also ceased to compete with them for the representation of the national will.

The extremists – or rather a section of them, for they fragmented constantly – were an important ally. Their very existence constituted a goad to reform. In fact, just as a nuclear deterrent is powerful only if it is not used, the revolutionaries were effective when they did not actually revolt – provided that they flicked the whip occasionally. The British government never saw Fenianism as a military problem. It was the problem of eradicating Fenianism without martial law or other surrenders of the 'civilised order' which proved intractable – especially when the acts of terror took place in Britain. The Disestablishment and Land Acts of 1869–70, scarcely conceivable half a dozen years before, were directly, though by no means solely, attributable to the Fenian disturbances after 1865. As Gladstone himself observed, the dynamitings, the killings, the arming of constables and the rest awoke in the British public as nothing else could have done some understanding of the depth of the Irish discontent: 'when the metropolis itself was shocked and horrified by an inhuman outrage, when a sense of insecurity went abroad far and wide', then Englishmen began to 'embrace, in a manner foreign to their habits in other times, the vast importance of the Irish controversy'.[1] 'Outrages' might horrify immediately, but given time they bred guilty consciences and conciliatory politicians. This brooding violence, this threat of blood to follow if concessions were too slow, was not all that Devoy had to offer his new friends. The apparatus of propaganda, publicity, popular organisation and finance built up through Clan-na-Gael and similar organs in the United States was a vital aid to the Land League and the Irish Party in the coming struggles.

The second element in the trinity of pressures was civil disobedience and mass subversion of the accepted order. These had been manifested in the 1830s in a rudimentary form, and inferentially constituted one of O'Connell's minatory weapons in 1843, but now they were seriously developed. The Land League, and later the National Land League, were designed to arrest evictions by boycotting or otherwise intimidating new tenants of 'cleared' land. Sporadic local violence and menaces had attempted the same at many times and places. But the Leagues were of a totally different dimension: firstly, because agricultural distress was deep and persistent after several bad harvests without protection from the new foreign competition; secondly, because the Leagues' organisation, largely manned by Fenians and ex-Fenians, was militant and efficient; thirdly, because the smallholders were more literate and less beggared than their counterparts of 1847, while their programme had taken a sharp, sudden, but permanent turn to the left in the mid-1860s; and finally because Irish-American money made prolonged resistance feasible by providing resources to support the worst-hit casualties. The movement had universal appeal and, given mass involvement, it was a short step from boycotting to fixing (unilaterally) acceptable rents and adjudicating tenancies – in short, to beginning to impose from below a new social and legal order. 'Make the ownership of the soil the basis of self-government,' Davitt had urged. Again, the government was presented with intractable problems: populations cannot be imprisoned or civility imposed by law.

None of this perturbation, however, was likely to win concrete concessions had it not been channelled into Parliament and deployed masterfully by Parnell. By 1879 Parnell had piratically seized control of the flaccid, directionless and disintegrating Home Rule party in the House of Commons, and begun to fashion it into an instrument of his own. Thus opened one of the great political performances of the nineteenth century. Though the scale was smaller, the duration shorter, and the issues less, Parnell's ascendancy can be compared without absurdity to Bismarck's. Like Bismarck, Parnell created a situation or series of situations in which he appeared to the relevant power groups to be indispensable. Parnell would not accept membership of the IRB or actually countenance violence; he would not tolerate clerical direction; he dictated to his parliamentary supporters; and he used the land agitation primarily to increase his bargaining power at Westminster. Despite all this, the Fenians, the church, the party and the Leagues – the four pillars of power in contemporary Ireland – rapidly concluded that they must acquiesce in his leadership at almost any price. In part, Parnell achieved his domination by balancing one force against another. In his first defiance of party orders and the official leader, Butt, he appealed over the heads of the gentry who composed the bulk of the Home Rule party to the mass of positive nationalists and of Fenian sympathisers whose attitudes had not hitherto been expressed in Parliament. In defying ecclesiastical censure by identifying himself with the first Land League, he staked a claim to peasant support where peasant feeling was most deep and lasting. It seemed hazardous for him at the start to trample on parliamentary propriety and play the demagogue. But in this early series of calculated risks Parnell identified himself with such powerful national moods and needs that he could defy 'respectable' Catholicity, lay and clerical alike, and eventually force it to join his bandwagon. And while seeming to bind himself to extremism, he really bound extremism to himself.

From 1881 on, he threw his weight (though only opportunely) against 'violence' and 'disorder'. This covert conservatism fitted his personal inclinations, furnished a *quid pro quo* for Gladstone's concessions and reconciled moderate opinion in Ireland to his leadership. As early as 1882, Davitt complained privately that Parnell spoke of anarchy like a minister introducing a Coercion Bill. Yet Davitt endured Parnell's equivocation even on such an issue as the Plan of Campaign. The party lieutenants were long aware of the hidden limits of Parnell's militancy, of his increasing neglect of political work and of his reckless liaison with Mrs O'Shea. Yet they endured all these, even (after some ill-concealed struggles) his foisting of her odious husband upon an Irish constituency in 1886. The explanation in both cases is, simply, the absence of access to alternatives. After 1881 the repudiation of Parnell would have broken the common front which presented the gravest threat to British domination since 1650. Parnell's political *raison d'être* was to provide both a focus for the various Irish aspirations and leadership above the factions. No one else was sufficiently independent of, yet touching, the many knots of Irish organisation. No one else possessed the requisite public personality, or the capacity to treat with British ministers on equal and mutually comprehensible terms. In Ireland, Parnell gave off a sense of boundless radicalism held temporarily in check. 'I have never attempted to set a *ne plus ultra* to the march of Ireland's nationhood and I never shall' epitomised the promise of unlimited advance which finally fastened popular support to his side. Yet he explained away such utterances, as best he could, in accepting Gladstonian Home Rule as a 'final settlement'.

There was perhaps no necessary contradiction. Parnell was in many ways a product (the less common 'hons and rebels' type of product) of a conventional English upper-class education; he personally favoured co-ownership of landlord and tenant rather than peasant proprietorship or land nationalisation; he knew little (though he spoke much) of industrial civilisation; and his real object was a new form of empire moderated by dominion status for the old dependencies. On the other hand, he possessed marked historical and political imagination. He not only grasped what was appropriate for and politically possible in the 1880s, but he also understood that things ripen and generations change. 'Finality' had to be ephemeral unless history stopped. It is not too difficult to visualise Parnell taking Griffith's or even Eamon de Valera's line in 1918–21, although in each case the role would have been played in a different manner, and in the second to a different conclusion.

The core of Parnell's power was the party, steadily developed from 1880 to 1885. Its central feature was the member's pledge, taken *before* he was elected, to abide by party decisions in the Commons. The election itself was certain in 80 per cent of the Irish constituencies once the Ballot Act had rendered voting secret, and the Reform Act of 1884 had so enlarged electorates as to ensure overwhelming Nationalist majorities. Party nominees were selected by a combined operation in which the professional management at the centre and the county conventions, where clerical and local influences were strong, came secretly to terms. No member rebelled after 1885. About half of them were supported to a greater or lesser extent from party funds; but whether financially assisted or not, all were controlled in their political behaviour by Parnell's Old Guard – McCarthy, Healy, O'Connor, Sexton, Dillon and William O'Brien. In turn, the Old Guard, whom Parnell consulted individually but not collectively, were subject to his decisions. For the first time in British parliamentary history, group discipline was absolute.

In the first phase, 1880–4, Parnell had more than thirty votes at his command; from 1885 on, he had at least eighty-five; and as far ahead as could be seen, the new system guaranteed this support ad infinitum. With one-seventh of the House of Commons under his control, certain to back, oppose or harry ministries as directed, Parnell had an efficient instrument for exploiting British party conflict. His extra-parliamentary auxiliaries vastly increased his purchase upon Parliament. The impression of agrarian war and revolutionary nationalism held sullenly in check always strengthened his hand. The acknowledgment of his leadership – in particular, his *national* supremacy – by the moderates and the church had the same effect for the opposite reason, namely, that British governments dared not throw over altogether their only possible sympathisers among non-Protestants. All this is not to suggest that Parnell's struggle to build the new Irish complex had been safe or easy, or that he did not have always to consider what the various elements of his support would not stand. The final debacle is proof enough of this. But the debacle also proved that only the most extraordinary pressures could shake his power, and that even then his grasp on Ireland could not be altogether broken.

From 1878 on, his power was growing fast; by 1882, no ordinary challenge was likely to disturb him; by 1885, he had acquired an almost Louis XIV-like domination. This domination, the very concentration of all nationalist, separatist and Catholic forces upon a single leader, and the electoral demonstrations of the impregnability of his leadership, were probably the decisive factors in inducing Gladstone and later the bulk of his cabinet and party to commit themselves to Home Rule. Parnell had, in the highest degree, political repose. His demands were rarely specific, but his purpose – to utilise all the inherent weaknesses of a modern liberal power holding another people in subjection – was unwavering. Parnell's dramatic downfall and the catastrophic defeat of the second Home Rule Bill in 1892 give a misleading impression of sudden failure after dazzling promise. In fact, the Parnellite decade profoundly changed the Anglo-Irish balance of power. It permanently changed imperial policy towards Ireland, as well as the social fabric of the island.

In 1880 landlordism was still substantially intact. In 1890, not merely had all the old objects of tenant right been achieved, but the process of land purchase for the establishment of peasant proprietorship was in flow. By 1890, even – perhaps we should say particularly – the Conservative Party was committed to a sustained attempt to undercut Irish nationalism by increasing productivity, improving education, redistributing population and engendering minor industry, and by democratising, and enlarging the functions of, local government. That a great British party should pledge itself to Irish self-government, or that a large, well-drilled Irish party could be sustained, or that the Irish nation could so discipline itself as to accept one leadership and follow complex directives *en masse* over several years would have seemed preposterous in 1880. None of these developments could be undone. But the great decade had also lessons on the other side. Three in particular were ominous. First, the wild Ulster reaction of 1885 to the prospect of Home Rule had revealed an obstacle over which even Parnell might eventually have fallen. Secondly, the meagre Bill of 1886 showed how very small a measure might be wrung from Parliament, and even that required the most explicit acceptance of the Bill by the Irish as 'a final settlement'. Lastly, the consequences of Parnell's fall brought out all too clearly the vulnerability of a movement which owed its coherence, its meaning and its life to a single man. Parnellism could not be institutionalised. The Parnellite concentration of forces was impossible without the hero.

Parnell's impress on Irish politics was still discernible in the twenty-five years which followed his fall. The party was broken in two (and later, three) in the 1890s, and even after the restoration of substantial unity in 1900, the old wounds never healed completely. The common front disintegrated: extremism returned to 'the ratholes of conspiracy', and the land agitation, except in the stricken west, died away. Alternative forces of great significance for the future – literary, linguistic, social, socialist and anti-parliamentary groups and ideologies – stirred painfully to life. But nothing could as yet displace the basic patterns of the 1880s; Ireland seemed still mesmerised by the Parnellite experience. But John Redmond, the faithful Parnellite who succeeded to Parnell's old position in 1900, could not simply take up the party's threads where they had been broken in 1890. The unmeasured personal bitterness which the split had released could never be recalled. The church, forced back into the foreground of politics by the first exigencies of organising anti-Parnellism, gained an embarrassing influence with that faction as well as unmerited obloquy among its opponents. It was not true that the priests had seized their opportunity to destroy Parnell and defame the radicals. They – like two-thirds of nationalist Ireland – had thrown Parnell over only when it was certain that his continued leadership would frustrate the avowed national objective. But the facts had long since been buried. Clericalism and anti-clericalism were more evident than ever before in Irish politics; and the paradoxical consequence of it all may have been not only that the bishops had a larger share in national leadership than they had enjoyed for forty years, but also that (perhaps to clear themselves of charges of conservatism) they now sometimes stood to the left of the party rather than the right.

In Parliament, the reunion of votes was far from being a reunion of hearts, and even the reunion of votes was incomplete: the Healy and O'Brien factions eventually reappeared. Moreover, the party had owed much of its original success to the shock of its initial impact upon the parliamentary system. By 1900, the system and the party had adjusted to one another, a process which robbed the latter of the last vestiges of its quasi-revolutionary character. The emasculation of the Irish Party had occupational even more than social causes. The routine of committee and similar bread-and-butter work in the Commons wore away its distinctiveness over the years. Besides, once resistance to Home Rule had been fixed and hardened in the Conservative programme, Parnell's original conception of a wholly independent party was vitiated. The Irish Party might still swear that it was totally indifferent to British politics and ready to make and unmake governments solely in accordance with Irish interests. But by 1900 it was only too apparent that for Home Rulers to make a Conservative government or unmake a Liberal one was simply to cut their own throats.

Finally, Redmond's leadership, representing as it did a compromise between warring Irish factions, was of a much lower order than Parnell's; nor did Redmond suggest, as Parnell had always done by the very nature of his personality, that responsible government for Ireland might be but the first instalment of larger gains. In fact, Redmond would have opposed anything beyond responsible government within the empire as strongly as he opposed the Act of Union.

C

'Let us have national freedom and imperial strength and unity,' he declared – from the heart. Contemporaneously, Griffith, the originator of Sinn Fein, described the Irish Party's activities thus: '103 Irishmen in the House of Commons face 517 foreigners . . . [on a] battleground . . . chosen and filled with Ireland's enemies'. Whatever reason might tell them, and however much the parliamentarian tactic promised, most Irishmen sympathised instinctively with Griffith's view, and recoiled instinctively from Redmond's *civis Romanus sum*. There was, therefore, a hidden dichotomy between the ultimate aspirations of the national leader and the led. Nor, indeed, would many members of either his party or the Catholic hierarchy have accepted Redmond's concept of dual allegiance as in itself desirable, or genuinely identified themselves, as he did, with any political structure which was British. These divergences were insignificant, though occasionally manifest, before 1910. But from then on, when Home Rule had at last become politically practicable, they began to count increasingly. Redmond was inhibited by his own beliefs from enlisting Irish militancy as an ally. This both weakened him in negotiations with the cabinet and gradually disenchanted Irish opinion with his methods and his ends.

The general elections of 1910 were a bitter disappointment to the Liberals. They lost heavily to the Conservatives, each party ending the year with 272 seats. But Redmond's highest hopes were fulfilled. The Irish Party, with eighty-four seats, held 'the balance of power'. Theoretically, this was the ideal Parnellite situation, even if it was inconceivable that the party would use its king-making powers to place the Conservatives in office. Moreover, not merely the Liberals but the fourth group, the forty-two Labour members, were pledged to Home Rule, giving in effect a 126 majority for the measure in the House of Commons. Finally, the Parliament Act of 1911 ensured that the House of Lords could only delay but could no longer destroy Home Rule, and that the latest date to which they could hold it up was the summer of 1914.

In several respects the 1912 Home Rule Bill fell short of Irish desires; but in the first flush of victory, it was the principle which seemed to matter. Here at last was the prize; it had cost forty years of toil, and even blood. Redmond's reception at the subsequent National Convention in Dublin was tumultuous; for the hour he belonged to the 'uncrowned kings' of Ireland. Certainly, the Bill was an advance upon the Gladstonian measures. Only the issues of peace and war, treaty-making and the imposition of new customs duties were reserved for the imperial Parliament, whither moreover Ireland was to send forty-two members, who might participate in all parliamentary affairs, and not merely those of Irish concern. It was still a far cry from dominion status. But representation at Westminster, and the eventual control, either partial or complete, of taxation and the police were vital advances upon the nineteenth-century proposals.

The Bill was devolutionary, or at most federalist, in tendency: it was not separatist. In introducing it, the Prime Minister, H. H. Asquith, made it clear that in his eyes the sovereignty of the imperial Parliament was not impaired. He spoke of a process of internal rearrangement of government within the British Isles, of which Home Rule constituted merely the first step. With such a view of Home Rule, the notion of partitioning Ireland was not entertained. For more than a generation four-fifths of the Irish constituencies had demanded Home Rule in terms of the whole island; it was a constitutional demand made persistently by a constitutional party; and the twentieth century had provided what the nineteenth century never did, an absolute majority in favour of the measure among the British members of the Commons. Nor did Asquith see himself as promoting Irish divisions. Given the over-riding imperial loyalty and imperial authority, why should not the claims of Irish Unionists, no less than Irish Nationalists, be accommodated by Home Rule, and why should the argument of administrative convenience have less force for Ulster than for the other provinces? This is not to say that the Liberal cabinet was unaware of the Ulster problem. Winston Churchill, Sir Edward Grey and Lloyd George were already advocating particular concessions to the north. But any move in this direction seemed unnecessary. The Ulster Nationalists were not a small minority. They constituted 45 per cent of the population of the province, and actually returned more Ulster members than the Unionists. Moreover, Redmond could not concede partition without being overthrown by his party; already he had severely tried its loyalty by his acceptance of the Bill. The Unionists equally opposed partition. The southern Unionists looked with terror on their fate, should they be unsupported by the north. The Ulster Unionists held to the strategy that their uncompromising opposition could destroy Home Rule for all.

Redmond's position in 1912–14 was that Ireland would accept 'a subordinate parliament' as 'a final settlement', and henceforth be loyal to the empire generally. He disliked the qualifications upon the Irish Parliament's powers over finance, public order and other matters. But he dared not press too hard for further concessions lest the Liberal cabinet postpone the whole measure or, more likely, exclude Ulster from its operation. On the other hand, he could not surrender what the Bill had already secured without endangering his leadership. He had, therefore, dangerously little room in which to manœuvre. If pressed to the extremity, he might be able to carry another parliament for Ulster subordinate to the all-Ireland parliament. But, politically speaking, he could not sacrifice 'Irish unity' and live.

Up to a point, his best ally was Sir Edward Carson, leader of the Ulster Unionist Party since 1911. Carson, by origin a southern Unionist, rejected partition outright. 'Ulster', he swore, 'will *never* be a party to any separate treatment.' Carson was taking it for granted that Home Rule was impracticable unless it covered the whole island. The whipping-up of northern resistance-to-the-death was designed to defeat the Bill in its entirety. By the great force of a passionate personality or of a consummate actor, he induced both the Ulster Unionist Party and the Conservative Party generally to adopt his strategy. It was one of the most extraordinary achievements of modern politics. The power of a great national party was harnessed to a provincial faction. A single *simpliste* analysis of a highly complex situation drove all others underground. Yet Carson was building on a miscalculation: Ireland, without Ulster, *was* a viable economic unit. Moreover, the Carson policy was perilous in that it tended to leave the Liberals without any other choice but to maintain their measure altogether or abandon it altogether. After all that had passed, total abandonment was inconceivable. It was in this sense, in keeping the Liberals behind the original Bill, that Carson, for a time constituted Redmond's friend.

Carson could scarcely have manipulated the Conservative Party so effectively were it not that after six years in the political wilderness and three successive general elections in which they had secured less than two-fifths of the seats, the argument for ruthlessness was strong. The new leader, Bonar Law, was meant to symbolise counter-attack; and 'Ulster' was the ground he chose, as much because he cared most deeply here as because it seemed the tactically wise selection. His forebears had been northern Presbyterians, and he himself had grown up in that nursery of power-winners, the Canadian manse. He was abetted by an interloper of another sort, F. E. Smith. Ridden by these demonic spirits, the Conservative Party in 1912 moved close to a position which a later generation might call 'fascist'. Law publicly anathematised the democratically elected government as a 'revolutionary committee seizing by fraud upon despotic powers'. Smith publicly declared that he would accept the consequences of war in Ulster 'though the whole fabric of the Commonwealth be convulsed'. Carson publicly announced that however often the electors might decide in favour of Home Rule, Ulster would fight regardless of their verdict.

What did all this mean? Would the Conservative Party have plunged at last into support of northern Protestant commandos, if fighting had really broken out between them and the British forces? Would the names on the Ulster Covenant have sprung up armed men, once bullets really flew and men died horribly? We can only guess. An Ulster in which an anti-Home Rule Army waged the same sort of campaign as did the IRA in 1919–21 – a few thousand guerillas on the run in an overwhelmingly sympathetic countryside – is not inconceivable. But it is difficult to speculate for long in this fashion without feeling that one is play-acting. Should we not ask, rather, was it ever conceivable that such a government as Asquith's would have forced this issue?

For Redmond, at any rate, this was the agonising question from 1912 on. To outward appearances, he had won Home Rule already; he had only to bide his time till the Lords' powers of delay were exhausted. But in reality his success depended on whether the Liberals would stand firm under menaces, or more precisely on Asquith's assessment of the genuineness of the Ulster threat. As late as September 1913, Home Rule still seemed safe. Asquith rejected an offer to attempt a compromise. He argued that even if Carson and Bonar Law were not bluffing, Home Rule would bring 'organised disorder but not civil war in Ulster'; whereas if Home Rule were abandoned, the rest of Ireland would be 'simply ungovernable'. Moreover, partition would not solve the problem even in the north, for even the four most Unionist counties had no less than 30 per cent of Nationalists in their population.

Perhaps Home Rule really was secure so long as the balance of fears, in Asquith's mind, was tilted in its favour. But before 1913 was out, a counter-army to the Ulster Volunteers was launched in Dublin in defiance of Redmond's wishes. This signalised a fatal weakening of Redmond's authority, and of the whole parliamentarian cause in Nationalist Ireland: the moving spirits of the new Irish Volunteers were clear Republicans, and the force was infiltrated by the IRB from its inception. It also meant that, with the sudden likelihood of war in Ireland between private armies, the Liberal cabinet listened more sympathetically to proposals of compromise. In the transformed situation, an old scheme of Lloyd George's that Ulster be exempted from the operation of the Home Rule Act for a number of years gained in attraction. The cabinet did not adopt it immediately, but neither was it rejected. The drift toward 'flexibility' had begun, with the Liberals already exerting oblique pressure on Redmond to surrender some of his paper gains. He could not hold out. If he resisted absolutely, he ran the double danger that Asquith would use this as a justification for postponement, and that the growing militancy at home would generate much more radical demands than the 1912 Bill could satisfy. Reluctantly, he agreed that any

Ulster county might opt out of Home Rule for a period of six years.

It is easy, in retrospect, to condemn Redmond and (for other reasons) the Liberal leadership for a concession which won nothing. But each had a reasonable case. Redmond could argue that he had kept – in the long run – the substance of 'Irish unity' (and in fact only four Ulster counties would have had Unionist majorities) and, equally important, that he had retained the Liberal alliance. Certainly, his concession led immediately to a Liberal resolve to force an amended Bill through. Former waverers such as Lloyd George and Churchill now turned on the leading Conservatives for preaching treason and sedition, and announced that 'these grave matters' would soon be 'put to the proof'. Conversely, when Carson rejected the compromise out of hand – 'give us a clean cut or come and fight us' – and forced the Conservative Party to follow his lead, he strained his position grievously. Behind the facade of Conservative unanimity and undiminished pugnacity, two serious splits were opening up: one between the frightened southern Unionists and the inflexible Ulstermen, the other between moderate and diehard Conservatives. The moderates feared that English opinion would soon come to label the Nationalists and the Liberals as the 'reasonable', 'conciliatory' parties. Unionist leaders (even Law) feared nothing so much as that some device such as county option would put them in the wrong, and present them to the world as wilful and surly bigots.

Thus the pendulum swung back toward Home Rule in the spring of 1914; in a real sense, the Lloyd George 'concessions' had turned the tables on the Unionists and forced them to the defensive. Their response was to raise the stakes. The Ulster Volunteers prepared for real war, most dramatically by running in 35,000 rifles and 3 million rounds of ammunition at Larne on 24 April 1914, while magistrates and other forces of public order stood by complacently. Again, Asquith weakened. Not only did he not retaliate in Ulster – and the root cause of all the Liberal troubles was their failure to tackle the problem of the northern Volunteers – he compounded his error by his handling, unhandling and mishandling of the Curragh business. In the end, he took over the War Office himself; as Ensor wrote, 'His followers supposed that this tokened a policy of firmness such as only a prime minister could put through: in fact, it heralded a policy of surrender such as only a prime minister could put over.' In short, when faced in 1914 with an apparent determination in Ulster (however British opinion might stand) to resist Home Rule by force of arms, the Liberal cabinet gave way.

Redmond was once more the victim. First, as the violence in the north went unchecked, counter-violence in the south mounted. The Irish Volunteers swelled to almost 200,000 in number, and Redmond was forced to take on the formal leadership of the movement. Like Asquith's action, this was a confession of weakness, not a measure of strength. Redmond was seeking desperately to establish some influence over anti-constitutionalism before it got completely out of his control. The second consequence for him of the new Liberal retreat was the Buckingham Palace Conference of July. Redmond was coerced into the weakness of further negotiations, after he had already bargained away some of his earlier achievement. Of course, the conference failed. Both Redmond and Carson denied that they were plenipotentiaries; and in a real as well as a formal sense this was true. Neither could have carried his followers with him on the only conceivable compromise, a partition of the island – Redmond, for obvious reasons, and Carson, because he could not have secured more than the four most Unionist counties at this juncture. Liberals and Conservatives alike were rescued from the now-terrible Irish embarrassment by the outbreak of the First World War, which, so to speak, enabled the impasse to survive. The Home Rule Bill reached the statute book in September 1914, but it was not to operate until peace returned, and meanwhile provision for its amendment was guaranteed.

Thus the original problems of 1912 were handed on intact to the postwar world. Throughout the long crisis, Redmond's statesmanship contrasted poorly with – the inevitable comparison – Parnell's. True, Parnell never had to face Redmond's worst difficulties: a Liberal Party without Gladstone, and Conservatives who followed rather than led the Ulster Unionists. But where Parnell had first outmanœuvred and then tamed and deployed the Irish forces of violence, Redmond first underestimated them and then allowed them to seize the initiative. Parnell projected a heroic form of leadership, Redmond that of the presider. No one took Parnell's measure; but it was apparent all too early that Redmond's reactions were predictable. It may be that Redmond was the more truly tragic figure of the two. But neither then nor now could the world at large, intoxicated by sensation and vicariously in love with power and will, understand such a judgement.

4
The New Nationalism

The fall of Parnell broke the pattern of Irish history as sharply as O'Connell's defeats and death had done nearly half a century before. This was not immediately obvious. The shell of Parnellism, in terms both of party organisation and of formal political objectives, covered nationalist Ireland for twenty-five years after the leader's rejection. But beneath and outside the shell, movements expressing other and often antagonistic aims began to grow. The staples of nineteenth-century political history, the parliamentary party, the doctrinaire Republicans, the militants, and the masses organised for land-wars, did not disappear. But in the interstices which opened up under the stresses of the 1890 crisis, and of the modernisation of Irish life, quite different organisations and objects thrust themselves outwards toward the light. Most were born in the heat or aftermath of Parnell's power, and their day was long in coming. But eventually they governed, or at least helped powerfully to shape, the development of Ireland at the most plastic stage of all, the years 1912–22.

Although these new forces may be very variously assorted, it is most illuminating to group them in three general categories: first, those concerned with the 'Irishing' of Ireland; secondly, those which attempted to comprehend and build upon emergent rather than traditional factors in Irish life; and finally, those which tried to subordinate the local issues to larger, more universal themes. In the first category three movements predominated: the Gaelic League, the Literary Revival and the Gaelic Athletic Association. All of them were launched in the seven years 1886–93, and all of them sprang from discontent at Ireland's drift toward British cultural and social forms. Parnell and Parnellism offered no resistance to such a tendency. When his London physician told Parnell that he would never have suspected him of being Irish, it was not merely his accent but also his entire manner, assumptions and forms of thought which marked him out as British. And how was the Dublin parliament of the Home Rulers' dreams to be conducted? Westminster *in parvo* seems much the most likely answer. The orthodox Irish Nationalist of the 1880s and 1890s was scarcely aware that a 'problem' of anglicisation existed. But as Douglas Hyde observed in 1892, 'the Irish race at present is in a most anomalous position, imitating England and yet apparently hating it. . . . It has lost all that they [the old patriots] had – language, traditions, music, genius and ideas. Just when we should be starting to build anew the Irish race and the Gaelic nation – as within our recollection Greece has been built up anew – we find ourselves despoiled of the bricks of nationality.' Certainly, in outward forms of life and expression, the distinctively Irish element was in decline in the last decades in the nineteenth century. It was under pressure from British modes and habits, and still more from mass culture in every form, the fruits of rapid communications and universal education.

The Gaelic League was intended by its author, Hyde – or so at least he proclaimed – to be a-political as well as non-sectarian, to be concerned solely with the nurturing and expansion of the Irish language. But Hyde failed to avoid politics, partly because his movement was deliberately infiltrated by extremists, and partly because such a movement implicitly encouraged the idea of a separate people. The League inevitably manufactured separatists. It also became a sort of school for rebellion, as well as an apparatus which knit sections of the middle and lower classes in the towns into a quasi-political association. The effects were profoundly important. Instead of binding Irishmen of all types and opinions together (as Hyde originally had hoped), it drove the wedge between north and south, between Unionist and Nationalist, deeper than ever. It gave new point and precision to Irish self-identity, externalising and symbolising what had hitherto been an inchoate aspiration in many cases. It helped to undermine the Irish Parliamentary Party, which bore to its dying day the impress of a pre-Gaelic generation. Not least – to look ahead – it created in advance an Irish Question with which the native governments from 1922 on wrestled, and still wrestle, without end.

The Literary Movement, like the Gaelic League, originated in the ascendancy, and was similarly conceived of as a-political at the beginning. In fact, Yeats positively denounced Irish nationalism insofar as it prostituted art in the name of politics, and spread shoddy literary and cultural standards. There was also in Yeats's mind (and perhaps to a lesser extent in Hyde's) a distinct antipathy to modern urban and industrial civilisation. Peasant life and language, the peasant's elemental nobility, stoicism and realism, were to be saved and cherished, to form a rock against materialism and mass values.

> John Synge, I and Augusta Gregory, thought
> All that we did, all that we said or sang
> Must come from contact with the soil, from that
> Contact everything Antaeus-like grew strong.

But once more it proved impossible to avoid entanglement with separatist politics. To preach nativism, and the retention or re-creation of social forms distinct from and antagonistic to those predominating in Great Britain, inevitably fed the flames of separa-tion and anglophobia. It is extremely difficult to evaluate the contribution of the Literary Revival to the ultimate insurrection and war of independence. Yeats himself asked inconclusively: 'Did that play of mine send out Certain men the English shot . . .?' Clearly, his movement furnished no framework of organisation such as the Gaelic League's. The Abbey and Coole Park could not be readily infiltrated. Nor were they obvious 'prizes' to be secured. Yet whatever its own purposes, the literary movement cultivated and shaped the separatist mind, not to say the type of highly-wrought romantic im-agination which flowered to a significant degree in the Easter Rising.

The third Gaelicising force, the Gaelic Athletic Association, differed strikingly in its origin from the other two. It was a mass movement, unintellectual and positively grounded in militant separa-tism from the outset. The GAA sought to insulate native from British sport by a system of exclusion and boycott. It was an applica-tion of the technique of the land war to a branch of ordinary life with the ulterior purpose of creating and maintaining a different national identity. Thus the Association was from the beginning what the League and the Literary Revival ultimately became – a mechanism which gave new substance, and day-to-day reality, to the concept of a distinct Irish nationality.

Strangely enough, over most of the nineteenth century, the distinct nationality of Irishmen had been assumed rather than defined or defended. Certainly, definition and defence were more urgently needed as regionalism declined fast in the British Isles in the last quarter of the nineteenth century. But the three Gaelicising move-ments were creating something new rather than buttressing the old. One ominous implication of this was the increase in the divisive forces in Ireland itself. A Gaelic Ireland, which spoke a different language, played different games and fostered a different culture, could only deepen the gulf between the north-east, which clung to the British patterns, and the remainder of the island. Most of all was this true of the Gaelic Athletic Association, which, especially in rural areas, also formed a network which touched in some degree or other a very considerable proportion of the population.

The next set of new factors, those working toward the modernisation of the Irish economy and Irish social practices, tended in the
opposite direction. The most significant of these ventures was the
co-operative movement initiated by Horace Plunkett in 1889.
Plunkett was no socialist. His objects were, in the most orthodox
senses of the terms, economic and moral: to render the Irish farmer
self-reliant and technically competent, and to call upon the state to
aid this work only when individual exertion had launched it fairly.
At first blush, nothing seemed more innocuous. But in *fin-de-siècle*
Ireland nothing was quite what it seemed. Plunkett was a Unionist
MP, playing a critical part in the conciliation ventures from the
Recess Committee of 1895 to the Devolution project of 1904. In his
own view, 'conciliation and conference' stood outside, or above,
normal political alignments. But to the conventional, Unionist and
Nationalist alike, it represented a rival movement which threatened
to undercut entrenched positions and established interests. Even the
co-operative and agricultural reform movements could not, therefore,
altogether avoid conflicts with nationalism and its opposites; nor
were these conflicts quite unreasonable, for economic miracles (or
even the promise of economic miracles) are also political events.
Thus Plunkettism went off at half-cock. But it did go off. Another
layer of ideology, another programme and another complex of local
organisation were added to the late nineteenth-century innovations.
Perhaps tragically in the light of later Irish history, the separatists
made no attempt on this occasion to capture or to utilise a movement
with separatist potentialities. A more certain tragedy, for themselves
at least, was the hostile reaction of the bulk of the Nationalist Party
to co-operation, technical improvement and the conference method.
It loosened their hold over large sections of Irish rural and clerical
opinion.

The aspirations to furnish Ireland with elements of a twentieth-
century economy were not confined to Plunkett's dream of a second
Denmark. A chauvinistic version of the same desires was the 'Buy
Irish' campaign, sustained by such influential journals as *The Leader*,
and more or less in tune with Griffith's Sinn Fein. Attempts of this
kind to promote Irish manufacture were much more economically
jejune than Plunkett's co-operativism, but at least they recognised
that political separatism, to be fully meaningful, implied economic
independence. The ulterior motive may have been nationalistic, the
cry for modernisation merely an incidental implication of the efforts
to increase Irish self-sufficiency. But it certainly coincided with
Plunkettism in envisioning a transformation of the means of production, distribution and exchange in Ireland.

A third stream – a mere trickle, in the event – was contributed by those Irish businessmen who, looking ahead, were ready to come to terms with Home Rule. An extraordinary example was Lord Pirrie, who dominated the Belfast ship-building industry before 1914. Dr Black explains his conversion to Home Rule as follows:

> He was interested only in having a stable political system within which he and other people could get on with their jobs; in other words, he believed in the liberal values of free enterprise and free trade – as what ship-builder or ship-owner at the turn of the century did not? Hence, the growth of his opposition to the Conservative and Unionist party can be explained by the repugnance to him of the doctrine of Tariff Reform, while his support of Home Rule arose from a belief that the continued government of Ireland from Westminster could be neither stable nor economical.[1]

Few Irish entrepreneurs reasoned so rigorously as Pirrie, or to the same political conclusions; but few could have been quite impervious to the promptings of economic realism. Business indulges sentiment only to a degree; ultimately its own survival and increase are more important. An attitude like Pirrie's was in several respects antithetical to those of the neo-Listians, or even of Plunkett. But again it met them on the ground of creating a viable, separate Irish economy.

Finally, other voices called for the subordination of peculiarly Irish to more universal interests, or at least pleaded for an acknowledgement of wider contexts and responsibilities. Our present preoccupations lead us to think first of Marxism, though it was but one of a host of supra-national nostrums before 1917. Certainly, James Connolly and some early trade unionists in Ireland saw Irish conflict essentially as class conflict (as indeed did Salisbury and Balfour), just as they saw British imperialism through Hobsonian or Leninist spectacles. Connolly, for one, saw Irish conflict as an inextricable portion of a general war, a war between capital and labour – whether in arms or otherwise was merely tactics – which already existed in Ireland. But this was but a local manifestation of the death struggle between the bourgeoisie and the proletariat the world over. In August 1914 Connolly, like many other socialists, 'Utopian' as well as 'scientific', expected the workers to prefer class to country. It was only when these hopes disintegrated that his internationalism wore thin. At the other end of the same scale, the last rising hope of the Irish parliamentarians, Thomas Kettle, tried to transcend the local and the temporary by placing the Irish struggle in the long context of Christian, or more exactly Catholic, Europe. It was (in his own phrase) the 'dream born in a herdsman's shed' which informed

Ireland's demand for liberty: the purpose of liberty was to restore her to her ancient place among the nurseries and bastions of European civilisation. Correspondingly, Kettle saw petty nationalism as only the initial step toward a United States of Europe. Neither Connolly nor Kettle evoked a sympathetic response in early twentieth-century Ireland. But fifty years later, in a world familiar with the notions of 'wars of liberation', Christian Democracy and European unity, their preaching may seem more relevant. At any rate, they heralded more spacious views in which Ireland's problems were related to great movements in the world. Even in 1910 they presented standing challenges to the conventional interpretations of the Irish Question.

The most significant of all the new movements was, of course, Sinn Fein. Touching several of the others, it was yet *sui generis*. Alone, it offered a complete political strategy. It differed radically, moreover, from any earlier plan of action. Although his personal inclinations were separatist, Griffith advocated dual monarchy, partly because of the successful precedent of the Austro-Hungarian Empire (or so he said), but also because the retention of British monarchical forms seemed indispensable if the north were to be conciliated, and if Irish independence were not to destroy Irish unity. Griffith's nationalism was as fierce as any Fenian's, yet he opposed violent revolution as both hopeless and wasteful. Parnell was Griffith's 'uncrowned king', to whom his emotional commitment was lasting, yet he detested to the day he died the bases of the Parnellite system: personal leadership (or, as we have it, the cult of the individual), and the final concentration of all Irish pressures in the British Parliament itself.

The three positive elements in Sinn Fein had appeared before in Irish history, but only in vague and inferential form. The first was the removal of all the Irish members from Westminster and their reconstitution in Ireland as a native parliament. The second was the assumption, so far as might be practicable from case to case, of executive powers by the new Irish body; to the extent to which this succeeded, British administration would become otiose and die of inactivity; ultimately the native 'state' might secure international recognition. Finally, Griffith looked to mass popular action, by civil disobedience, passive resistance and voluntary involvement in the native system, to sanction the new departures and to stultify British power. Sinn Fein, therefore, anticipated, if it did not positively inspire, some of the characteristic devices of anti-colonialism in the middle decades of the present century. It was also destined to supply some of the prerequisites of success in the Irish situation of 1917–21. But all this was for the future. In 1905 Griffith's was only one of a chorus of voices crying up new wares to replace the old and tried.

Like most of these voices, it was unheeded by the great majority, and mocked by many.

There are, then, two Irish histories for the three decades 1886–1916. One is the history of the parliamentary party (or rather parties), of land and local government reform, of the ebb and flow of the fortunes of Home Rule – accompanied by the constant, if now faint, contrapuntal theme of conspiratorial republicanism. This history engaged almost all contemporary attention. But behind it lay another history, of slowly fermenting agitations and experiments. These were, by and large, the ripening forces of the future. The explanation of this hidden but profound change lies in many contemporary developments. A social and political vacuum had been created in Ireland by the recent blows to the ascendancy. Irish Protestants had had to come to terms – and their responses were various – with the probability that Ireland would become, in some form or other, independent. Parliamentarianism was discredited, and seemed *passé*, over much of the United Kingdom, and not least in Ireland. Violence was not only practised, but was even preached in Edwardian England. Most significant of all perhaps, Great Britain's economic decline was under way, while simultaneously the British Isles were being knit more closely into a single economic unit, in which the pace of urbanisation, of rural depopulation, of rising living standards and standardised living habits quickened amazingly. All this was the breeding ground of the doctrines and organisations which we have enumerated. Not surprisingly, their significance was concealed before 1914. They looked forward to a different world from that which had fashioned the great nineteenth-century themes. By the same token, it may be observed that the issues which they raised have not yet been finally resolved. The relationship of nationality and language; the meaning of national art; the practicability of remaking a lost popular culture; the degrees of independence of, and subordination to, the international market which make a strong economy; the reconciliation of political independence and supra-national political trends; the very nature of a separate race – all these raise questions hanging over Ireland still, sixty years later.

Meanwhile, the ancient cause of physical force suddenly revived in Ireland on the eve of the First World War. Strangely enough, although the IRB had survived and in fact enjoyed a major reorganisation and a minor revival after 1900, it was from British rather than native sources that violence returned to Ireland. The immediate cause of the return of militarism in the south was the formation of the Ulster Volunteers and the 'chatter' about armed resistance among English Conservatives. The Irish Republicans ostentatiously welcomed Carson's move, and not altogether with tongue in cheek. They professed to admire his 'realism', that is, his contempt for parliamentary processes and numerical majorities: deep was calling to deep. More practically, they saw that his action had provided them with an opening for turning Irish nationalism back again towards more violent courses. The establishment of the Irish Volunteers (the counter-organisation to Carson's force), in November 1913, was virtually stage-managed by the IRB. Using leading members of the Gaelic League, especially Eoin MacNeill, as 'front men', the Brotherhood intended to control the new body through Sean MacDermott and a very recent and most important convert, Patrick Pearse. These two occupied key positions in the first executive. What all this really signified was that for the first time in over forty years, the advocates of violence in Ireland had a real prospect of capturing, or at least of influencing significantly, the mass movement of Irish nationalism.

In fact, their early hopes were disappointed. MacNeill and other moderates acted independently, and so far from breaking with the parliamentary party, invited its co-operation. Redmond seized the chance, as he saw it, of neutralising this danger on the left. He insisted that half the Volunteer executive should be composed of his party nominees. This scarcely enabled him to control the movement, especially when various sections acted autonomously, in (for example) gun-running. But at least it reduced to very small proportions the number of the IRB men on the executive, and still more in the rank and file, which had grown to almost 200,000 after Redmond associated the party with the movement. It was the outbreak of the Great War which saved the day for extremists. When the Volunteers divided on the issue of support for Great Britain in the conflict, the rump of intransigents, a mere 12,000 strong, was of course more malleable material for the conspirators. Within a month of the outbreak of the war, the Supreme Council of the IRB summoned a secret meeting of important members of the recalcitrant (now named, the Irish) Volunteers, which determined upon an armed rising before the fighting in Europe was done. The IRB was still a fragment, working surreptitiously within a fragment: MacNeill, the commander-in-chief of the Irish Volunteers knew nothing of, and would certainly have opposed, their plan. But because of the secession of the main body of moderates, and the smallness and militancy of the remaining core, the Brotherhood's design became at last practical politics.

A second consequence of the formation of the Ulster Volunteers, no less dramatic in the change which it caused in Anglo-Irish history, was the demoralisation of the Crown forces in Ireland. In particular, the central administration in Dublin Castle and the Royal Irish

Constabulary lost heart and nerve. The near prospect of Home Rule, from 1912 onwards, would have induced, in any case, a slackening of will. But it was the unimpeded enrolment in and arming of the north, culminating in the Larne gun-running, which administered the *coup de grâce*. At first sight, this may seem contradictory: did not Carson's challenge ensure, at the very least, that the Union would not be lost without a struggle? The explanation lies in the precedents set by the Liberal government's passivity in 1912–13. It was impracticable for the Liberals to deny to their allies in the south what they had permitted their enemies in the north. Consequently, the formation of private armies by the Nationalists proceeded practically unchecked in 1913–14. It was the first time since the enactment of the Union that the south could form an armed force without hindrance. The most significant consequence of the shootings at Bachelor's Walk, on 26 July 1914, was not that they provided new martyrs for the militants, or that they let blood flow once more for Irish freedom (and these things were indeed important), but that the assistant commissioner of police who had taken action against the nationalist gun-runners was censured and dismissed from the service by the Irish secretary. The lesson was not lost upon other Irish officers of the Crown. From this demoralisation derived the extraordinary spectacle of an Irish Volunteer army, patently 'disaffected' and 'rebellious', drilling, marching and manœuvring in broad daylight, at a time when the United Kingdom was embroiled in terrible war, and her government empowered with terrible authority by the Defence of the Realm Act and similar emergency legislation. Nor was the emasculation of the Irish executive halted by the Easter Rising, or even by the Lloyd George government in its wartime phase. The militants were scarcely less effective in organising 'subversion' in 1918 than in 1915. The war ended with Dublin Castle palsied, and the RIC on the threshold of disintegration.

The other Irish form of violence in 1912–14 was industrial, and virtually confined to Dublin. Again, the source was external – in this case, the example of British labour unrest in 1910–11. The Citizen Army began as a strike defence force, became a workers' revolutionary brigade and ended – practically, though not formally – as an auxiliary of the IRB. It, too, drilled openly, and preached revolution almost unrestrained. But a mere handful were involved. Doubtless, historical institutes in the Soviet Union reverently dissect the pathetic elements of this little band. But only the eyes of faith (or of prophecy) could see Connolly's movement as anything but peripheral to the major conflict. Still, it was not unimportant for the future that bridges should have been thrown across the gulf between political and economic radicalism in Ireland, even if – or perhaps particularly if – the traffic flowed in only one direction. Connolly's subordination of his own plans for revolution to those of the IRB in 1916 did not end the struggle for revolutionary socialism in Ireland. It reappeared on the fringes of extreme republicanism at several junctures between 1922 and the outbreak of the Spanish civil war; and yet again in the later 1960s. But each time the old pattern has been repeated: abstract nationalism has eventually consumed every Marxist cuckoo in the nest.

The Great War was seven weeks old before Redmond took the fatal step – as it seems in retrospect – of committing Ireland to support the cause of the Allies unconditionally. His initial policy, the use of the Irish Volunteer forces only to defend Ireland's shores, and with no Oath of Allegiance to the British Crown, had the support of even the extreme nationalists. But in an extraordinary *volte face* on 20 September 1914, Redmond abandoned all qualifications and ordered the Volunteers to 'account for yourselves as men not only in Ireland itself, but wherever the firing line extends, in defence of right, of freedom and religion in this war'. To what extent he was moved by his own underlying imperial loyalty, or by War Office pressure, or by political calculations about British opinion, or by secret understandings with the Liberal government, is unknown. What is certain, however, is that Irish nationalism was ultimately offended. Redmond's prestige and the great weight of the party's organisation still generated such momentum that almost nine-tenths of the Volunteers followed the new lead, many to the extent of hieing to the Flanders trenches. But as the casualty lists grew longer, and war weariness and war cynicism developed, Redmond's breach of the historic principles of regarding not British, but Irish sentiment, and regarding not the common causes but the basic enmities of the two countries, brought inevitable retribution. Since no general election was held between 1910 and 1918, the progress of disenchantment with the Nationalist Party cannot be accurately charted. Until a serious rival emerged, moreover, mass opinion had no alternative to choose. But the speed with which Sinn Fein advanced after the initial hostile reaction to the Easter Rising amply demonstrates how support for Redmond had been eroded by the end of the second year of the war.

Before Redmond's declaration of 20 September 1914, a small group dominated by the IRB had, as we have said, met secretly in Dublin and resolved to stage a revolution. They intended to use for this purpose whatever sections of the Volunteers they could induce to join them. The task was simplified by the division in the Volunteers after 20 September. The hard core who repudiated Redmond's lead were, almost by definition, more or less militant separatists. Even so, the majority of them might have opposed the rising had they had foreknowledge of its occurrence. The three leading officers in the organisation, MacNeill, The O'Rahilly and Bulmer Hobson, conceived its function to be strictly defensive – in particular, to fight only if an attempt were made to enforce conscription upon Ireland. This meant that the Easter Rising had to be prepared without their knowing – still more, without the rank and file of the Volunteers knowing – what was really afoot. The difficulties of the conspirators were extraordinary. Apart from keeping the principal officers of the Volunteer Council in the dark, Dublin Castle had to be deceived, Connolly prevented from acting independently and the landing of German arms and the outbreak of the rebellion co-ordinated. Although the second and third hurdles were in the event successfully negotiated, the first and fourth presented such difficulties that the Rising went off at half-cock, with only a fifth of the expected revolutionaries in the field and no significant provincial (let alone German) assistance for the Dublin rebels. To have risen at all was, in the circumstances, an achievement; but this was only the beginning of the wonders.

As has been said a hundred times, the Easter Rising came like a bolt from the blue, surprising equally all the established protagonists in the Irish imbroglio. A week of fighting in Dublin, ten days of almost desultory executions, three thousand 'rebels' shipped to Great Britain for internment, and it was all over – apparently. Of course, all parties were shaken out of the strange trance which had descended once the Home Rule Bill was passed (with assurances, of course, that it would never come into force unchanged), and Redmond had taken his fateful stand in September 1914. Asquith had now to revise his strategy of shelving the entire issue till the war ended. Lloyd George, destined to be prime minister before 1916 was out, was freed to resume 'negotiating a settlement', a process to be crowned, after a devious decade, by the legerdemain which clinched the Treaty on the night of 6 December 1921. Redmond and Dillon, the Nationalist leaders, could no longer pretend that the Republicans were mere paper patriots; they could not but recognise that parliamentarianism must now bear fruit soon or perish. The Ulster Unionists exclaimed that the Rising had confirmed their prophecy that Irish nationalism would turn, must by its very nature turn, to separation, treason and a bloodbath. But none of them saw the Rising as more than a danger signal, a warning of the unpleasant consequences of continued delay or further concession, as the case might be. Their existing attitudes were revitalised, but they failed to understand that all had 'changed utterly', or to place the event in a general historical perspective.

But the significance (not to say the very language and symbolism) of the Rising is missed unless the long past is taken into account. In particular, it should be borne in mind that in the struggle for reforms which had begun on 1 January 1801, four great modes of exerting Irish pressure upon the 'mother-country' predominated. These were pressure through a parliamentary party and the British political system; passive resistance and civil disobedience; the gradual super-session of the existing British government in Ireland by a native substitute; and armed insurrection. It was the last of these, almost exclusively, that 1916 represented: that is to say, the pressure was exerted upon a very narrow front. But it is also true that 1916 represented the first demonstration of armed force since 1801 which deserved the name of insurrection: 1803, 1848 and 1867 had been not only total but also ludicrous failures. No one, however, could dismiss 1916 as a street brawl or a cottage siege. Moreover, the Rising has been justly termed a Fenian or IRB rebellion; and the IRB had ultimately derived from the French Revolution of 1789. The historical accident that doctrinaire Irish nationalism was born in the 1790s had stamped Republicanism and Romanticism upon its face for ever. The basic French concept of the Sovereign People, and the Jacobin gloss that it was the party alone which discerned the people's real will, were faithfully repeated in all subsequent Irish revolutionary movements – or rather in *the* Irish revolutionary movement, as men like Pearse, claiming an apostolic succession from Tone and Emmet, would have said.

To understand 1916, this derivation must be remembered, and we should further bear in mind the internal logic of the revolutionary ideas. If the movement was the rightful interpreter and determinant of the people's will, and if the Irish Republic was not a distant objective, but a living, though hidden, reality, then it followed that the legitimate government of Ireland was vested in the movement's leadership, and that the British forces in Ireland were an enemy army of occupation holding down a subjected though unconquerable land. The IRB and the Volunteers might seem half-crazed millenarians to the worldly-wise, but they saw themselves as responsible in their own generation for expressing the eternal truth of Ireland's independence. It was, if one likes, all *Alice*, with hedgehogs and flamingoes for balls and mallets. But our own century has shown how easily the fantasy may change places with the fact. At any rate, this interchange was the final result in Ireland, with new myths, new orthodoxies and new passports to place and power arising from the ashes of the old. To pursue the *Alice* image further, 1916 may be regarded as the moment when doctrinaire nationalism begins to pass, at last, from inside the Looking-Glass to without. The Proclamation of Easter Monday (the term itself is redolent of authority) declared that the long usurpation of government by a foreign people had not destroyed, and never could destroy, 'the Irish Republic as a Sovereign Independent State'. The signatories constituted themselves a Provisional Government. The Irish nation was mobilised to 'prove itself worthy of the august destiny to which it is called'. Mere words and aspirations perhaps – but to assert them in arms and blood was already, in the circumstances of the day, to clothe them with some reality.

The Irish War of Independence, of which the 1916 Rebellion constituted the opening act, was at once modern and antique. At least in terms of the British Empire, it was the pioneer and exemplar of future independence struggles and anti-colonialism. But it was also a struggle between white men, and (Connolly, the Citizen Army and the collectivist items of the Democratic Programme of 1919 notwithstanding) a struggle, as we have said, innocent of Marxist or even serious socialist implications. Perhaps the time or the race or both were out of joint; but whatever the cause, socialism, always a minor element in Ireland, was enslaved in 1916 to purely nationalistic objectives. The most acute of contemporary observers noted the essential conservatism of the rebels. Yet no capitalist or even propertied or religious interests were being fought for; in this respect, other tempting comparisons, with the Dutch and the American revolts, fall short. The most meaningful historical context for the Rising still remains that of the French Revolutionary tradition. Despite all its prospective and innovatory aspects, despite, equally, its place in the age-old catalogue of colonial disaffections, the least misleading categorisation of 1916 is as the final flower of the Romantic Nationalism of the nineteenth century.

The actual execution and, so to speak, style of the rebellion carried romanticism, we might even add chivalry, to extraordinary heights. The revolutionary idiom of this century – sabotage, terrorism, assassination, in fact all that promised any hope of military or quasi-military success in contemporary Irish circumstances – was not employed in 1916. Instead, uniformed 'armies' marched through the streets to take up their positions; Pearse stepped out on to the pavement to read his Proclamation before a shot was fired; the revolutionaries invoked God's blessing and prayed that they would not be dishonoured by 'cowardice, inhumanity or rapine'; and the codes of war were almost pedantically observed. Everywhere, in the language, the conceptions, the literary remains and even the official documents of the Rebellion, the hands of poets and rhetoricians can be detected. In fact, a sort of lyricism explains the very character of the enterprise. Pearse had said a year before, 'Life springs from death, and from the graves of patriot men and women spring living nations': 1916 was not expected to succeed; it was expected to fill patriot graves; 'while Ireland holds these graves Ireland unfree shall never be at peace'. Chesterton oversimplified but was essentially right in saying that Pearse and some colleagues desired to be martyrs in the ancient and literal sense – that is, they hoped not to be victorious but to bear witness.

It was at this point that the other and neglected modes of exerting Irish pressure became significant. It was a gross though general error of the time to name the Easter Rising a Sinn Fein rebellion. Sinn Fein had differed radically from revolutionary republicanism. It was nonviolent; it sought no republic; rather than insurrection, its immediate plan was for withdrawal of all Irish members from Westminster and their reconstitution as an Irish parliament. Apart from their common contempt for the ineffectuality of the Irish Parliamentary Party and for the inadequacy of Home Rule as a solution, the extremist movements were mutually exclusive. But they were also mutually dependent. Sinn Fein would have been nothing, and its visionary, Griffith, no more than an interesting curiosity, had not the drama and emotional repercussions of the Rising melted the moulds in which Irish mass opinion had been fixed for almost a quarter of a century. On the other hand, mere insurrection was a *cul-de-sac*. What was to follow, beyond fresh sacrifices in other generations? In fact, revolutionary republicanism desperately needed something like the Sinn Fein *modus operandi*, and the Sinn Fein emphasis upon moral force, civic organisation and the legitimation of radical courses by popular sanction at the polls, if any further headway were to be made.

The junction between the two forces, initiated in the fighting of the by-elections after the rebellion, was consummated at the close of 1917 when de Valera became president of both movements, thereby creating in effect two arms, military and political, of a single national front. Fusion of several modes of Irish pressure had always proved more effective than concentrations upon one medium. The new separatist association, although differing in its elements, resembled in its essence the amalgam of parliamentary party, popular organisation, and demi-Fenianism which Parnell had hammered into a single instrument in the 1880s; 1916 had demonstrated to the world at large the earnestness, intransigence, nobility and force of militant Irish separatists. But this was only one prerequisite of success. Victory at the polls was also necessary, both to destroy the incumbent Parliamentary Party and to demonstrate that absolute separatism was the steady passion, not of a scattering of enthusiasts, but of the people. Moreover, electoral success was a necessary preliminary to an independent national assembly, and an independent assembly was a necessary preliminary both to international recognition of the state and to the effective organisation of a native legal and administrative system to supplant 'the foreigner's'. This last in turn opened the door to the pressures of mass disobedience and passive resistance.

One form of pressure remained unused, that of a parliamentary party upon Westminster. The price of this abandonment was grievous. Would the north-east corner have been effectively secured for the United Kingdom if the Government of Ireland Bill of 1920 had had to meet the fire of Irish parliamentary opposition? Would the Coalition Government have been able to defend its repression in 1919–21 effectively? Would Tyrone, Fermanagh, South Down and South Armagh have been lost ultimately to the south? The questions tumble out endlessly. But to have allowed parliamentary representation at Westminster would have destroyed the *raison d'être* of separatism. This apart, however, over a vast area of politics, the historic type of violent, conspiratorial republicanism was bankrupt in 1917, but Sinn Fein rich in expedients. The romance of the revolution may have been over, but its realisation could begin when the activist strategies were commingled.

When the third stage of the campaign was reached early in 1919, and armed conflict was resumed, it was upon precisely the opposite principle to that of the Easter Rising. The new phase was of guerilla war, burnings, ambuscades, executions, reprisals and intimidation. *Pace* Mr Dooley, armies may fight in the open, but nations must do so behind rocks and trees. Now commonplace, war by un-uniformed men, melting into the civilian body when not in action, was then a startling innovation. But a second rising would have been entirely pointless, not to say impracticable. If military pressure were to be added to the rest – indeed, if world attention was to stay riveted on the little island – there was no other way. Moreover, it is at least arguable that the other modes of pressure being employed in 1919–21 could not have been sustained without the carrot of guerilla victories and the stick of terror. But it was, none the less, an ironic finale to the brave flags set streaming and the brave men set marching upon Easter Monday.

To borrow from an enemy of it all, the Rising was, therefore, not the end, nor even the beginning of the end, but certainly the end of the beginning. A line had been drawn across the page, cancelling an interminable tale of compromises sought and lost. The initial rebellion must be regarded as a portion of a process, rooted in crude historicism, though catalystic in altering the future, if the historical reality is to be understood. But it was also a magnificent event, self-enclosed, self-defensible, imperishable, as Roncesvalles; a thing of men's imaginations, made from and creating literature. It may be the rhodomontade that first arrests us, but it is the ultimate seriousness of the actors which holds us in the end.

> We know their dreams; enough
> To know that they dreamed and are dead;
> And what if excess of love
> Bewildered them till they died?

Moreover, as on many previous and many future occasions, from the executions of Allen, Larkin and O'Brien in 1867 to the death of Sean South in 1957, the blood-sacrifice struck a chord in the Irish race-consciousness, deeper than prudence and calculations. Even William Martin Murphy, the notorious enemy of Parnell and of the Irish socialists, was not exempt. After the Rising, 'He admitted that at first he felt bitter against the insurgents [because of the burning of his property] but finding the Tories gloating over the executions and imprisonments "every drop of Catholic blood in my veins" surged up, and he began like others to pity them.'[2]

Ironically, the 1916 Rebellion gave Redmond – temporarily – new hopes and brighter prospects. Asquith, visiting Dublin in May, acquired fresh resolution; the pendulum was swinging back again. In imagination, the prime minister cast Redmond as an Irish Botha (forgetting that the Afrikaaner's status as a war-hero rendered the parallel most inapt) and conceived of himself as repeating Campbell-Bannerman's feat of 1907, plucking the flower, safety, from the nettle, danger. Significantly enough, however, Asquith, though driven to conclude that the 1914 moratorium on the Irish problem could not be sustained, still thought in terms of the 1912 Bill. As with English statesmen generally, he did not understand the change which had been wrought when a Republic was proclaimed and sealed in blood, when indefeasible and *present* nationhood had been asserted. It had been shown that men would die for a sovereign nation. But who would throw away his life for cautious Devolution?

At any rate, the new policy of May 1916 seemed to promise immediate concession. When the Irish chief secretary resigned after the rebellion, he was not replaced: the alternative was an Irish executive responsible to an Irish government. To carry this through, Asquith would accept the immediate operation of the Home Rule Act as soon as 'the different parties in Ireland' came to agreement. The negotiations were left to the supreme broker, Lloyd George, who eventually succeeded in forcing Carson and Redmond to accept common terms – but only on the basis of contradictory assurances to the two. Carson was given to understand that the six north-eastern counties would be permanently excluded from the operation of the Act; Redmond, that their fate would be decided at an imperial conference after the war, at which all the dominion premiers would be present. Carson had thus surrendered permanently both the old

United Kingdom and three Ulster counties; Redmond had surrendered – temporarily, he supposed – two counties, two cities and several other districts with Nationalist majorities, as well as the basic concept of a united island. The cat was put among the pigeons when Lloyd George reported his 'success' to the – now Coalition and therefore part-Unionist – cabinet. The ministry split so violently – several Conservatives denouncing it as 'a concession to rebellion' – that the scheme had to be abandoned. Worse still, a Unionist peer exposed its provisions (or more exactly, its provisions according to the Carsonite version) in the House of Lords. The upshot was that both Redmond and Carson revealed what had been promised them, each declaring that he had been grossly deceived. To Redmond's protests against the cabinet's chicanery, Asquith replied by refusing to apportion blame 'for the breakdown of the negotiations. . . . The important thing is to keep the negotiating spirit alive.' He knew his man: Redmond – it might be his epitaph – could not stop parleying, though now, if ever, was the moment to break decisively with the British system and withdraw his party *en bloc* from Parliament.

Asquith himself fell from power in December 1916, before 'the negotiating spirit' could bear more fruit, but his successor, Lloyd George, naturally continued so congenial a policy. Moreover, to do nothing – or perhaps we should say not to appear to do something – would have been disastrous. Sinn Fein candidates defeated Nationalists at three by-elections at the close of 1916 and the beginning of 1917: it was as much in Lloyd George's interest as in Redmond's to check this trend immediately before constitutionalism rotted entirely in Ireland. Moreover, the British government, desperately short of manpower, wished to extend conscription to Ireland; but without some *quid pro quo* it could not be applied. Most serious of all, Britain was by now dependent upon American support for her war effort, and this would be imperilled unless there was, at the very least, some show of concession to Irish nationalism. It was the combination of these pressures which produced Lloyd George's 'offer' of May 1917, which issued finally in the setting up of an Irish Convention to hammer out an agreed settlement in Dublin in the following July.

The Convention was a strange agglomeration, nearly a hundred in membership. All Irish political parties, including Sinn Fein, were invited to send representatives; so, too, were the main churches, commercial interests, trade unions and county councils. Lloyd George guaranteed that he would adopt its report if there were 'substantial agreement'. It was a riskless undertaking. Who was to decide what constituted 'substantial agreement' but himself? How could so heterogeneous a body devise an agreed procedure, let alone a solution? Did anyone really believe that Ulster Unionists and doctrinaire Republicans could ever find a common formula? In fact, the Convention represented a mere variation on the tactics employed by the British government since mid-1914. These were, essentially, to abdicate direct responsibility for Ireland and to throw the onus of reaching a compromise upon the Irish antagonists: both the Buckingham Palace Conference and the negotiations of 1916 fit this pattern. At least, these tactics bought time, and never was time worse needed than in mid-1917. The Irish situation was frozen again, for at least six months. Meanwhile, Irish-American opinion was lulled by the illusion of activity, and the initiation of the Anglo-American military alliance correspondingly facilitated.

Despite his experience at Buckingham Palace and in the other negotiations with Lloyd George, Redmond readily accepted the Convention. Clearly, the sands were running out for him; now or never Sinn Fein must be challenged, before its grip on Irish nationalist sentiment closed. In the event, Sinn Fein was perhaps the prime beneficiary of the venture. By boycotting the Convention, it gained in the general estimation when, inevitably, no agreement was reached, and the causes of compromise and negotiation were proportionately discredited. A more practical advantage was the release of the Republican prisoners, incarcerated in Great Britain after the rebellion, as an initial gesture of goodwill when the Convention opened. This made possible the thorough reorganisation of both the political and military arms of the extremist movement without serious hindrance from Dublin Castle. On the other hand, the Convention aggravated the divisions and conflicts among the parliamentarians. Redmond and Dillon differed seriously; the Catholic bishops proved intransigent; *frondeurs* such as William O'Brien or William Martin Murphy added to the confusion. Meanwhile, the Ulster Unionists, forced to attend against all their inclinations and completely bound by the directives of the Ulster Unionist Council, remained suspicious and inflexible from first to last.

Of course, there was no agreement. The great divisive issues were three: the exclusion of the six counties; control of customs; and defence. In many ways, it foreshadowed the course of the treaty negotiations of 1921. Yet in some respects, the Convention produced significant advances. First, the Nationalist claims were gradually crystallising into something quite beyond Home Rule. As the significance of defence and customs in the proceedings indicates, dominion status was emerging as the aim. Not only would this have gone much farther towards satisfying Irish separatist sentiment; it was politically and constitutionally a much more viable form than the ambiguous condition of the 1912 Bill. Secondly, during the course of the Convention, the southern Unionists abandoned their outright opposition to Home Rule and moved quite far toward accepting quasi-dominion status for Ireland. Gradually, they had come to recognise that some change in Ireland's constitutional position was inevitable, and the Convention had produced reassuring guarantees for their property, religion and political representation. Finally, and most important from Redmond's standpoint, the Ulster Unionists were largely separated from their former political allies. The new programme of the southern Unionists was contingent upon a united Ireland in which they could rely on their fellow Protestants in the north. But the Ulstermen concentrated upon saving their own skins, upon the permanent exclusion of the north-eastern counties from any new arrangement. To the southern Unionists, and to many English Conservatives, this appeared as a callous 'betrayal' of their brethren; and the Ulster Unionists were also anathematised (not least by English Conservatives) for destroying all hopes of a negotiated settlement, at a time of grave national crisis when the empire desperately needed peace in and manpower from Ireland. Isolated and now depicted as self-centred and even disloyal, Ulster Unionism seemed in a weaker position in 1918 than perhaps at any stage since 1885.

Redmond died on 6 March 1918. He had spent his last months of life in a desperate struggle to hold the Nationalist elements together, to keep the Convention in being and, above all, to induce the British government to act as a government, to assume some responsibility for what was happening in Dublin and to throw its great weight upon the side of settlement. In his final bitter days, he realised that nothing would move Lloyd George to take the necessary action. In death, if not in life, he matched Parnell: his tragedy was classically neat. Yet, even as he died, the pendulum may have been swinging back once more to his side. The dominion objective was taking shape; the conflicts among Irish Unionists and between British and Ulster Conservatives were increasing. In the three Irish by-elections of the spring of 1918, the trend of 1917 had been reversed and Sinn Fein candidates defeated by Redmondites in every instance. It was not inconceivable that, even at this late stage, the Nationalist Party could have contained and eventually rolled back the Sinn Fein menace. Certainly the current omens were good. But whatever the chances really were, they vanished within a few weeks, dissipated by an action of the British government. This was the assumption, on 16 April 1918, of power to enforce conscription upon Ireland. The government could have hit on no device more certain to destroy all hopes of an Irish settlement – nor one more wanton or worthless, for these powers were never used. As Churchill said, 'We had the worst of both worlds, all the resentment against compulsion and in the end no law and no men.'

The first result of the Conscription Act was the withdrawal of the entire Irish Party, under Dillon's leadership, from the House of Commons. This action, which the Nationalists had threatened off and on for over forty years, marked the beginning of the end of parliamentary method. The essence of the original Sinn Fein programme had been precisely this step, to be followed by a reassembly of the delegates in Ireland; and Dillon's move blurred the traditional distinction between Nationalists and Sinn Feiners. (As we have seen, it also weakened, in some respects, the entire Irish agitation, which henceforth lacked the additional purchase which parliamentary advertisement of grievances and parliamentary bargaining had furnished, more or less, since 1830.) The next stage further injured the Nationalists. In the anti-conscription movement launched immediately in Ireland, Dillon represented but one of the three political groups which were involved (the others being Sinn Fein and the O'Brienites), and two other great forces, the trade unions and the Catholic hierarchy, equally embroiled themselves, or were embroiled.

At first sight, it might have seemed that the old popular front, so powerful under Parnell's over-riding authority in the 1880s, had been restored, and that Dillon might renew the genuinely national leadership which had been lost in 1890. Instead, it was the militants who seized the initiative. De Valera devised the anti-conscription pledge, with its significant reference to the Act as 'a declaration of war upon the Irish nation', and its clear call to the Irish people 'to resist by the most effective means at their disposal'. It was de Valera also who bearded the bishops, and secured their public and unequivocal approbation. The last touches needed to ensure the elevation of Sinn Fein to the summit of the national resistance were supplied by the British government. Together with its satellites, Sinn Fein was proscribed as a dangerous body, and on the basis of an imaginary German plot nearly one hundred of its leading members were imprisoned. This was 1917 all over again, except that now Sinn Fein possessed the added lustre of being the prime mover in organising and sustaining the anti-conscription movement, which appealed simply but profoundly to all Irish feeling. It was also 1917 once more in that British repression, though quite sufficient as an irritant, was so restrained that the covert organisation, arming and training of guerillas could continue; and several of the most important military (as against political) leaders, chief among them Michael Collins and Cathal Brugha, escaped arrest. Then 1917 was yet again repeated in that the by-elections of the summer and autumn of 1918 resumed the chain of Sinn Fein successes over the Nationalists. Conscription proved to be the Irish Party's *coup de grâce*; the last hope of recovery was gone. In the general election at the end of 1918, they won only two seats in open contests with Sinn Fein candidates, a terrible conclusion to almost forty years of mastery.

Sinn Fein had had a long run of fortune, and their luck continued in the general election. The franchise system (still unchanged) secured them over two-thirds of the Irish seats, although in the seventy-nine constituencies in which they were challenged, they received less than half the votes cast. They seized the opportunity provided by the return of seventy-three Sinn Fein members to Parliament – somewhat airily described as a declaration 'by an overwhelming majority, [of the people's] firm allegiance to the Irish Republic' – to ensure that there would be no turning back. Those members not in prison or in hiding assembled in Dublin on 21 January 1919, where they confirmed the existence of a Republic, asserted that British administration in Ireland was 'foreign' and illegal, and elected a new, 'legitimate' government from amongst their ranks. This was unmistakably revolution, yet neither side was prepared immediately to resort to arms, or to close all doors to negotiation. The Dail had met openly, and even after its unilateral declaration of independence it was not proclaimed an unlawful body. The Irish Volunteers had begun sporadic guerilla attacks upon Crown forces, but the Sinn Fein members did not yet sanction them or publicly approve; the party's programme of action, so far, involved no more than an attempt to substitute its own civil rule for the existing government in Ireland, and the winning of international recognition for the new state at the Peace Conference of Versailles.

The situation changed decisively in April 1919 when, as on two earlier occasions – the Sinn Fein convention of 1917 and the anti-conscription meeting in 1917 – it was de Valera, more than any other man, who altered the course of events. By then the government had released the Sinn Fein prisoners, and they tacitly permitted de Valera (technically an escaped prisoner since February) to attend the second sitting of the Dail. Here he was elected president and proceeded to designate a cabinet of nine. Most important of all, he introduced a motion which, in effect, licensed the violent assaults upon the police forces and other Crown agents in Ireland. From now on war was inevitable, and by the end of 1919 the IRA offensive had already reduced the effectiveness of the RIC and weakened the government's control of rural Ireland significantly. Dublin Castle's response – the proclamation of twenty-seven counties and the mass arrests of hundreds of known (and accessible) Sinn Fein sympathisers – was patently insufficient, and Lloyd George was forced to try another tack and attempt to wrest the initiative from the Republicans at the beginning of 1920. For almost two years they had set the pace, seizing successive opportunities to consolidate their hold on Ireland: 'The stars in their courses fight in favour of the Sinn Feiners,' T. M. Healy wrote. Now a more difficult phase was beginning.

In fact, the cause of the Republic had suffered, almost unnoticed, a grievous setback before 1920. The original strategy had centred on securing international recognition and bringing external pressure to bear on Britain to accept the new Irish 'government' as a *fait accompli*, for if this were achieved, the details of the constitutional relationship of the two islands might be negotiated with some measure of give and take. But the Irish bid to be recognised internationally at Versailles failed completely. Further, it was rejected personally by Wilson. The Republicans had regarded the United States as the *deus ex machina* which would force the solution which they wanted on Great Britain. Now their basic plan was in ruins. A second, and even heavier, blow fell early in 1920. Lloyd George at last determined upon a positive Irish policy, which consisted essentially of a major counter-offensive against the Republican guerillas and a Government of Ireland Act creating two Irish parliaments, for the twenty-six and the six counties respectively. This last probably spelt ultimate defeat for traditional Irish nationalism, although its full significance was concealed until the Boundary Commission was wound up in 1925. In 1913 the Ulster Unionists had prepared a Provisional Government for the north to seize power when the Home Rule Bill reached the Statute Book. Now they were presented with the same self-government which they had originally threatened to proclaim. It was not quite the Union; it covered only two-thirds of Ulster. But it was a fundamental guarantee against coercion. It is significant that the British government did not press seriously for a truce in Ireland until the Northern Parliament had been formally established in June 1921. Thus before the fighting was halfway through, the Republicans had probably lost half their battle. The Government of Ireland Act made it almost certain that *both* full independence and suzerainty over the whole island were unattainable: a choice would have to be made. Perhaps this was the underlying truth of the situation since 1885. But not until the 1920 Act was passed, and a Home Rule government installed in the one corner of the island which opposed it, was the Unionist position quite impregnable. The conclusion of Ulster's struggle since 1885 against national independence was in keeping with all the wry paradoxes of our story.

Meanwhile, the other arm of Lloyd George's new policy enjoyed varied fortune. Its failure was not absolute. From the beginning of

1919 until the early summer of 1920, the war had gone very much the rebels' way. Not merely had the RIC been driven back to the larger villages, but their intelligence section had been practically destroyed by the execution (*anglice* murder) of most of the principal agents; at the same time, an indigenous legal and administrative system had superseded British government over much of nationalist Ireland. The balance of Irish fear, as well as the balance of Irish sympathy, was tilted deep in favour of the Irish Republican Army. Already the British forces, not to add the RIC, had met terror with counter-terror, with burnings, looting and random killing. None the less, the increase in 1920 of the British army in Ireland to 50,000 men, and the recruitment of thousands of special armed police (the notorious Black and Tans and Auxiliaries) in Great Britain, had certainly checked the disintegration of British rule.

It is very difficult to strike a military balance-sheet for the last year of the war, from the summer of 1920 to the summer of 1921. One can scarcely say that the position of the IRA improved. The new repression was much more brutal and efficient than the earlier counter-terror. When the truce came on 11 July 1921, Sinn Fein had less than three thousand men 'in the field', and was desperately short of arms and ammunition. More serious still perhaps, the incessant British reprisals, involving the destruction of many million pounds worth of property and an increasing disregard for human life, must have worn down the will to resist among the general population. On the other hand, the British strategy was self-defeating. During much of 1920–1, the government threw the reins over the horse's head, tacitly abandoning control of its Irish forces: the evident calculation was that counter-revolutions could not be made with rose-water; that terror must be out-terrored; and that the less the actions of the forces of law and order were supervised, the sooner would the 'murder-gang' be destroyed.

But in the long run the official outrages alienated rather than satisfied British opinion. The government's use of censorship and propaganda (both techniques immeasurably improved by wartime experience) made it difficult for the Sinn Fein version of what was happening in Ireland to obtain a hearing. The absence of Irish representatives at Westminster was also a sore loss; the systematic use of parliamentary questions and debates on official policy might have crippled the counter-revolution. But gradually the government's reputation sank, in Great Britain no less than abroad. 'The whole world', as Chesterton wrote, 'thinks that England has gone mad'; and in England itself the practices of repression began to be condemned not merely by the parliamentary opposition (Labour and Asquithian Liberal), but also by independent Tories such as Lord Robert Cecil, independent ecclesiastics such as Davidson of Canterbury and independent organs such as *The Times*. English mass opinion was excited by such testaments of the reality of Irish feeling as Terence MacSwiney's seventy-four-day hunger-strike in Brixton prison: immense crowds followed his funeral procession in London no less than Cork.

Thus by mid-1921 British support for the government's Irish policy had weakened markedly. If the IRA could have been smashed immediately – by whatever means – doubtless the victory would have covered a multitude of sins, as the later cases of the Mau Mau in Kenya and the Malayan Communists suggest. But after nearly two and a half years of fighting, Great Britain was as far away as ever from complete success. In March 1921 a single engagement at Crossbarry, County Cork, issued in eighty-six British casualties as well as the loss or destruction of much equipment. Two months later, the Dublin Customs House was burnt down in daylight in an action which involved, directly or indirectly, several hundred members of the IRA. By June, the government had reached the conclusion that the pacification of Ireland required the Boer War methods of great 'sweeps' across the countryside, and chains of blockhouses, which might involve an additional 100,000 men at an additional cost of perhaps £100 million per annum. On the eve of the truce, then, Lloyd George was faced with the choice of throwing much more men, blood and money (and the last was not un-important) into the struggle or attempting to negotiate a peace.

There were considerable difficulties in the way of the second course. One was the power of the Unionist party in the Coalition: they would cry out against 'betrayal', all the more since their southern Irish brethren had already suffered cruelly for the Union; they might even destroy the ministry. Another was the official theory that the IRA was an 'army' of common bullies and assassins, and the Sinn Fein 'government' a criminal conspiracy built upon intimida-tion. On the other hand, it was increasingly a question whether British opinion would tolerate a continuation of the conflict, let alone treble its intensity and deepen the national disgrace. And if it were decided, as the current Irish secretary urged, to fight on until 'the last revolver' was plucked 'out of the last assassin's hands', what would be gained? Southern Ireland would have to receive self-government in some form or other, in the end. In short, the balance of advantage was decidedly in favour of negotiation.

The right moment, from the British standpoint, was when Home Rule for Northern Ireland had been safely harvested; and the right means of revealing publicly the government's change of front was a royal appeal: loyalists would accept from the Crown what they rejected from any other source. It was singularly apt, therefore, that the British public should have been prepared for peace by a passage in George V's speech (which Lloyd George had had a hand in composing) on 22 June 1921, when he opened the new parliament for Northern Ireland: 'I appeal to all Irishmen to pause, to stretch out the hand of forbearance and conciliation, to forgive and forget. . : .'

Thus was initiated the process of preliminary negotiation which issued three weeks later in a truce. In mid-1921 Sinn Fein had no prospect of military success in any ordinary sense. The real prize for which the IRA now struggled was British public opinion; and to have rejected the proffered armistice at this juncture might have loosened rather than tightened the Irish grip upon their objective. Moreover, Sinn Fein held out successfully in the preliminary discussions against the surrender of its arms as a precondition of the truce, and de Valera safeguarded his negotiating position by asserting in the early correspondence that peace was quite unattainable if 'Ireland's essential unity' and 'the principles of national self-determination' were set aside. On this note the fighting came to an end, and the contest was transferred to the fields of dialectic and diplomacy. The Irish proficiency, alas, lay in the first of these fields rather than the second.

For two months after the truce of 11 July 1921, Lloyd George and de Valera manœuvred for position. The immediate problem was to find a mutually acceptable formula for the peace talks. Great Britain could not allow that an independent Irish state existed already; the Irish could not accept the existence of imperial sovereignty. Through several meetings and much correspondence between the two leaders the respective presuppositions collided monotonously. At last a saving phrase was found, and the issue defined as 'how the association of Ireland with the community of nations known as the British Empire may best be reconciled with Irish national aspirations'. Blessed imprecision: each party could plausibly contend that 'association' would not necessarily derogate from the sovereignty which it already enjoyed. Moreover the formula recognized – at least implicitly – that because of geographical contiguity, to say nothing of economic ties, Ireland could not be 'foreign' to Great Britain in the same sense as Portugal or Denmark.

Much has been made of the difference in political quality and experience between the British and the Irish delegations, which first met for the peace negotiations in London on 11 October 1921. Certainly, the British principals, Churchill, Chamberlain, Birkenhead and above all Lloyd George, were the master politicians of their day, even if the leading Irish delegates, Griffith and Collins, showed unexpected capacity as negotiators. But as important as the abilities of the respective delegates was their standing *vis-à-vis* their governments. Lloyd George was his own master – and what master ever had a better servant for such work? – and could pursue a predetermined strategy. Griffith and Collins lacked both authority and clear instructions. In the absence of de Valera, who refused to attend the conference, come what might, the Irish delegation was instructed to refer all significant issues to the Dublin cabinet for decision. Meanwhile, they did not know exactly to what ends they should work or what minimum was acceptable to their Dublin colleagues. Thus the Irish began the conference under a heavy disadvantage.

De Valera's conception of his own role, and his previous experience of the national movement, may have led him to emphasise above all else the maintenance of Irish political unity. A common enemy and a state of war had hitherto repressed the marked divergences in aims and attitudes among the revolutionaries, but the prospect of peace immediately revealed the ideological divisions in Sinn Fein. He may have wished to buy time in which to produce another of his comprehensive, healing formulae when he let the delegation leave for London without precise instructions or either of the intransigent Republican ministers, Stack or Brugha, in its ranks. He was at work upon a new formula, External Association, which might kill two birds with a single stone – maintain the national front intact, and secure a constitutional status which would sufficiently reassure the British without offending Irish Republican susceptibilities. Perhaps de Valera was as much concerned with the national front as with a treaty. At any rate, his struggle to keep the factions under him united may help to explain some factors otherwise mysterious. Among them is the extraordinary failure to consider seriously the limits of possible British concession. Here the governing factor was the British cabinet's dependence upon Unionist support both in the House of Commons and in the country. This alone ruled out formal separation, even for 'non-external' purposes. Equally curious was the failure to consider seriously whether the IRA was in a condition to renew the war, or whether the Irish people were prepared to endure more blood and tears. The reality of Irish intransigence in the negotiations ultimately depended upon the answers to these questions; yet, so far as can be seen, they were left quite in the air. Thirdly, de Valera and his cabinet failed to consider seriously the implications of Northern Ireland's new security – a constitutional government of its own – which rendered it practically safe from a unilateral British disposal of its territory.

The treaty negotiations involved four main areas of conflict: first, fiscal and economic autonomy; secondly, executive and military autonomy; thirdly, constitutional autonomy; and finally – eternally

D

– Ulster. On the first two issues, the Irish delegates gradually won the day. When they secured full control over customs, tariffs and economic policy in general, their victory was symbolic rather than material. The Irish economy was, if not altogether dependent upon, certainly geared to the British economic system. But the symbol was important. Fiscal autonomy was an essential element in the idea of national independence. The equivalent was true of the untrammelled control of one's own judiciary, police, administration and army. Here again the Irish secured all, or almost all, of what they needed. The only significant qualifications were the ultimate appellate jurisdiction claimed by Great Britain – the right of appeal to the Privy Council from all Irish legal decisions – and the British right to retain certain naval bases, two on the Irish southern coast and one in Lough Swilly. The first qualification seemed, in 1921, to be a necessary consequence of dominion status. The second seemed an inevitable concession three years after a world war in which Great Britain's survival had depended to a considerable extent upon the use of Irish ports from which to conduct the anti-submarine campaign. The Irish delegates had successfully resisted many other British demands for strategic safeguards, including various uses of Irish soil for military purposes, and it was even arguable that the British naval bases buttressed Irish independence – in the short run. Towering over all else was the prospect of the evacuation of its Irish barracks by the British army, and of its Irish offices by the British administration. To Collins this in itself sufficed to mark the end of 'the seven hundred years' of occupation.

It must not be supposed that the British concessions – one might even say capitulation – in the first two areas of dispute came all at once. They were the product, apparently, of long and difficult bargaining. Some were held up by Lloyd George until the final night of the conference, obviously to retain a *quid pro quo* with which to match the sacrifices which he demanded of the Irish. These last lay in the field of constitutional autonomy. The key problem, as it seemed at the time, was whether and to what extent Ireland should recognise the British Crown. For each party, this was the decisive symbol: vital for the British, if any remnant of imperial sovereignty were to survive; vital for the Irish, because they saw the Crown as the emblem of their servitude. The conflict was irrepressible, partly because an oath of allegiance to some authority or other was required of all members of constituent assemblies, and partly because the same authority, by convention, accredited representatives abroad, signed passports and generally externalised the state in its dealings with the world at large. It was, in the end, the Irish who gave way, though not quite in unconditional surrender. This Irish concession was Lloyd George's *chef d'oeuvre* as negotiator. On the final night of the conference, 5–6 December, he presented his antagonists with the immediate choice of war or peace. Selected stage props – trains and destroyers on the ready to bear the news, and alternative letters written in either sense – helped to create an illusion of urgency. It was in a feverish atmosphere that the Irish finally accepted British sovereignty. Lloyd George had succeeded in his principal objective. Dominion status was his minimum demand; he could not hope to carry any larger concession in either his cabinet or the House of Commons.

But his victory was qualified and, in the long run, pyrrhic. The Irish delegates secured an oath which set out the primary 'allegiance' as being to the new Irish Free State, and only secondarily promised 'fidelity' to the British Crown. This was, constitutionally, a distinct 'advance' upon the current practice in the dominions, where the oath was simply one of allegiance to the king, *sans phrase*. Moreover, the Irish had sensibly avoided a precise definition of dominion status. Instead, they tied Ireland's powers and rights to those which other dominions – in particular, the most independent, Canada – might enjoy from time to time. Clearly, the dominions' advance in constitutional status was not yet spent, and the Irish were now guaranteed a place upon the escalator. Moreover, they themselves could speed on the disintegration of the imperial ties. Lloyd George had taken a perilous step in forcing a state, bitterly hostile to Great Britain, to stay within the boundaries of the empire. Canada and South Africa were politically divided countries, but each contained powerful British sections. The Irish Free State would be practically united in anglophobia. In an imperial system which depended ultimately upon mutual sympathy and consent, and was correspondingly weak and unspecific in formal organisation, the Irish had considerable scope for destructive operations.

In the years 1922–39, they seized every opportunity to cut the imperial connection; and both their attitudes and their legal triumphs changed the whole spirit of the empire. Thus, the Irish surrender and the British triumph on the constitutional issue were by no means as complete as they initially appeared. Griffith and Collins were ultimately justified in arguing that they had won 'the freedom to win freedom', to whatever limit the separatist impulse might require. They might also have argued – though in fact a curious silence was observed upon the matter – that some shadow of imperial allegiance, some obeisance to the British Crown, was indispensable if the north-east were ever to be joined politically with the remainder of the island; that the treaty in fact represented the ultimate concession to separatist feeling which was compatible with any hope of Irish unity.

The last major issue at the conference, Ulster, was handled disastrously by the Irish. Past experience suggested that it would prove the least tractable and the most confused of all. Yet it was far from the forefront of the discussions. Instead, the Irish delegates concentrated upon defence, finance and, above all, constitutional relations. Part of the explanation of their aberration was Lloyd George's control of the course of the proceedings. Lloyd George had long before prepared his checkmate: with a Northern Ireland parliament in being, he could always disclaim sole, or even prime, responsibility for the fate of the north-eastern counties. His second precaution was the procuration on 12 November of a secret undertaking from Griffith that he would not refuse to sign a treaty *merely* because of disagreement upon Ulster. Lloyd George had assured Griffith – doubtless truly – that he needed such an undertaking at that juncture to prevent a Unionist repudiation of negotiations which already threatened to produce large concessions to the 'disloyal' Irish. In the event, he used this document to most effect, not in soothing his Unionist colleagues, but in forcing Griffith to sign a treaty. Having already agreed in substance to the remainder of the terms offered on 5 December, Griffith was suddenly confronted by his own self-denying paper. Once he adhered to his original undertaking, the pressure upon his colleagues to concur was great, and in domino fashion they fell one by one.

Lloyd George achieved this result by dangling before the Irish eyes the prospect of eventual Irish unity through a commission to adjust the border between north and south. Naturally the Irish were tempted by the prospect of one-third or more of the northern territory being incorporated in the Free State, with the further assumption that the remaining fragment would prove 'non-viable', and finally fall in with the main body of the island. It was this combination of hope, fear, pressure and illusion which caused the Irish delegates to endorse partitioned Ireland in the end. In the Boundary Commission clause, they neglected to take (or insist upon) two seemingly obvious precautions, neutral international adjudication and clear instructions to the adjudicators as to the principles upon which territory should be transferred. Instead, they accepted a commission composed of one British, one Northern Ireland and one Free State nominee, and a phrase which left the commission free to determine the border upon practically any criterion which they wished to choose. The blunder was due partly to the inexperience of the Irish delegates, and partly to the fact that the issue came to the forefront only at the eleventh hour, which in turn derived from de Valera's desire to 'break the negotiations' – if break there had to be – upon the Ulster question. In short, the Irish were hoist with their own petard. If they had carried the day in the first two fields of conflict, and gained much more than was apparent in the third, they failed catastrophically in the last without even realising that they had been outmanoeuvred. Strangely enough, it was not for this failure, but for their backsliding in the abstract regions of Crown and empire, that they were immediately and angrily repudiated by so many of their fellow Irishmen.

5
The New State

Ireland, in many respects the pathfinder of anti-colonialism in the British Empire, was nevertheless remarkable for its fidelity to British models after independence. Both the forms and activity of central government were practically unchanged, and still more extraordinary, the British parliamentary and party systems were substantially repeated. This last was in direct contrast to what was to happen later in Africa, where in general the several parties of the last colonial days coalesced into a single party as independence drew close or was attained. In Ireland independence was achieved through a single party which thereupon broke in two. The emergence there of a purposeful opposition of the traditional British type appears to have been accidental. But Ireland had been conditioned for so long to British political practices and presuppositions (which, indeed, the Irish themselves had done much to shape) that a totally new type of party structure would have been difficult to envisage.

The two-party system in the new state originated in the Dail cabinet meeting of 8 December 1921, when the treaty was at last approved by a majority of four to three. There were never any hopes that the British conventions of cabinet solidarity and confidentiality would be observed on this occasion. The president, de Valera, not only repudiated the majority's decision publicly; he also named the diehards, Brugha and Stack, who supported him. Hence, in the ensuing Dail debate upon the treaty, conflicting policies were urged by the two sections of the cabinet. Moreover, the issue of acceptance or rejection of the London agreement was clear-cut. A choice was unavoidable, and like the Reform Bill controversy in 1831–2, the proposed treaty polarised the members inexorably. De Valera evidently expected to carry the day in the Dail. His surprise at the result – a majority of sixty-four to fifty-seven in favour of accepting the treaty – was said to have been apparent. Single-party government was at once in difficulties.

The pro-treaty leaders attempted to restore the status quo by proposing that the existing cabinet should remain in being, while their particular faction carried out the next steps toward ratifying the treaty. De Valera, spurning a course in which he would sit enthroned upon the ruins of his own policy, countered this proposal with one which was still more extraordinary. He offered himself for re-election to the presidency on the understanding that his new cabinet would be entirely composed of *anti-treaty* ministers. The declared object of this manœuvre was to maintain a government absolutely committed to a Republic until 'the Irish people' determined whether or not they would surrender a Republic for a Free State. De Valera was rejected by the Dail; and Griffith, elected in his place, proceeded to form first a pro-treaty cabinet for the Dail and then yet another government. He was bound to do so because the treaty demanded that a Provisional Government, to carry it into effect, be set up by the 'parliament of Southern Ireland'. This second ministry was headed by Collins, and about half its members were also ministers of the Dail cabinet; Griffith himself, however, was not a member of the Provisional Government. The evident purpose of this strange dualism was to keep the Dail undefiled by British claims to supremacy, and to prevent a lasting breach developing in the Sinn Fein party.

It was not yet certain that a lasting breach would develop. The anti-treaty group, knowing that they would be defeated at the polls, struggled to postpone a referendum, while the pro-treaty group, pressed by the British government, wished to proceed at once to a popular decision on a new, treaty-based constitution – a course which would also serve their immediate political interests. This conflict was not in itself enough to break the party; nor, technically, was the holding of a new general election on the same day as the proposed treaty was to be considered by the electorate. By the most curious of all the curious expedients of the first half of 1922, the facade of a national front was maintained by apportioning candidates from a 'panel' of pro- and anti-treaty Sinn Feiners, divided in exactly the same ratio as before, sixty-four to fifty-seven. Probably it was anticipated that substantially the same Dail would be returned. Other 'parties' were allowed to put forward candidates, but few expected them to be successful. No one seems to have considered at this stage what type of parliamentary system would be established, but it was probably assumed that an essentially one-party Dail would re-emerge, moderated perhaps to some slight extent by special economic interests.

If this was in fact the general Sinn Fein expectation, it was soon disappointed. The plan for preserving, or rather recreating, party unity failed because a third force, the Republican wing of the army, entered the field and denied the legitimacy of the Dail now that a majority of Dail members had voted for acceptance of the treaty. This group, which represented about half of the active 'soldiers', constituted yet another form of government in Ireland by declaring allegiance only to its own army council. 'Do we take it we are going to have a military dictatorship?' O'Connor, the leading army rebel, was asked. 'You can take it that way if you like,' he answered. Thanks to extraordinary shifts and restraints, this repudiation of the Dail's authority did not lead to a final, open breach between the pro- and anti-treaty factions until after the general election on 16 June, although it made such a breach inevitable. The Republican army would never submit peacefully to the Provisional Government, and the anti-treaty politicians would never throw over an army dedicating itself to the Republic.

A secondary cause of the failure of the one-party system was the surprising success of the non-Sinn Fein candidates at the election: they won thirty-four seats in all, only two less than the anti-treaty candidates and only twenty-four less than even the pro-treatyites. This introduced what was long to be a feature of the new parliamentary situation, that about one-quarter of the seats would be lost to the major parties. To some extent, the new mode of election – by proportional representation – promoted this sort of centrifugalism. But it was not an all-powerful tendency. Because of the large number of three and four (as against seven, eight or nine) member constituencies, the larger parties still had enormous advantages. Roughly speaking, in 1922 (and ever since) it took nearly twice as many votes to elect a candidate outside the two main parties as one who belonged to either of them. The other significant factor working for diversity of political groups was the concentration of the main parties upon constitutional, at the expense of social and economic issues. This induced the strongest and most distinctive sectional interests, the farmers and labour, to seek their own representation. Not that a majority of farmers or trade unionists in 1922 or at any later time supported their own sectional parties; but enough of them have done so throughout to deny some seats to the principal contestants. Thus, it was soon clear that one-party government was doomed, and that even the two-party system would be modified by the existence of lesser groups and independent representatives.

Even the results of the election of 16 June did not seem to contemporaries *necessarily* fatal to the ultimate reunion of the two Sinn Fein factions, although the facts that a higher proportion of the pro-treaty than of the anti-treaty Sinn Feiners on offer were returned, and that all the non-'panel' members favoured the treaty, rendered it most unlikely. But when, within ten days of the election, the

Republican forces precipitated armed conflict in Dublin and the long-threatening civil war eventuated, no one could hope any longer that Sinn Fein would be reconstituted. So long as the rival armies merely menaced each other, de Valera could regard himself as standing between the opposite poles of mere majority rule and military despotism, of a British dominion and a naked Republic; after all, at this stage the Republican army accorded him no more authority than it did the perfidious Provisional Government. But when the guns spoke, no middle ground was left; de Valera had to declare himself. He proceeded to describe the treatyites as those who had yielded to English threats and the rebels as 'the best and bravest of the nation', and to enlist himself and throw the support of his faction to the side of the new revolutionaries. From this moment onward, it was mostly a matter of time (although it was also a matter of the most tortuous and pedantic progress) until, in October 1922, de Valera's Republican deputies declared that they alone constituted the 'true' Dail Eireann. The next step was to elect de Valera 'president', to provide him with 'cabinet ministers', and to secure the blessing and the allegiance of the IRA.

This phase of 'anti-Pope' and 'anti-church' lasted less than twelve months. By May 1923, the armed resistance of the IRA was broken; the pro-treaty government would not come to terms with the Republicans, and de Valera had no choice but to capitulate unconditionally. By this time, the treaty had been ratified and the new Dail had settled down to regular business without the Republican deputies. The Farmers' Party and most of the independent deputies supported W. T. Cosgrave's government, and it was left to the small Labour Party of seventeen to provide the official opposition. De Valera's capitulation of 1923 was, however, physical rather than moral. For the next four years he continued to repudiate the Dail. None of his Republican deputies would take their seats, partly because this would have involved an Oath of Allegiance to George V. On the other hand, although the moral or metaphysical existence of the 'Republic' was still insisted on – somewhat halfheartedly – the pretence of a rival government was tacitly abandoned. De Valera's lieutenants met periodically, but these were probably desultory and dejected proceedings, which not even the members themselves conceived of as 'cabinet meetings'.

From 1918 to 1923, de Valera's political choices had proved unhappy. In the first two years after the Easter Rising, his performance had been flawless. He had disengaged himself from the IRB, established moral as well as formal ascendancy over the Volunteers in prison by sheer force of leadership, and then produced the two formulae which, respectively, fused Sinn Fein and the

Volunteers, and placed the combined movement at the head of the anti-conscription struggle. There followed, however, a series of unfortunate decisions, beginning with his precipitate departure for the United States in 1919 and ending in his precipitate enlistment in the dissident Republican army in July 1922. In between, he had offended the old Irish-American leadership by refusing to commit himself to a Republic, and lost the support of the American national parties by standing out for a Republican commitment. He had remained in the United States when he should probably have been in Ireland, and in Ireland when he should probably have been in London. He had asked the impossible of his plenipotentiaries; and the 'impossible' – to stage-manage a 'break on Ulster' – might well have proved valueless had it been achieved. He had denied the right of the negotiators to negotiate to a conclusion, as in the end he denied the right of majorities, whether in the Dail or among the electorate, to determine the final issue. He – the careful student of Machiavelli – had ended at the mercy of the zealots. Now, in 1923, began the long and complex process of disentangling himself from the forces of violence, reconstituting himself as a parliamentarian and exploiting the provisions of the treaty to supply its own defects.

Meanwhile, Cosgrave's government steadily established both its own authority and the new state. In August 1922, when Griffith and Collins died within a few days of one another, when de Valera was steeling himself to proclaim a rival government, when armed conflict was still spreading while the wounds of the former fighting remained unhealed, few would have expected that within a year the Free State would be secure and practically, if not theoretically, unchallenged. Yet this was achieved. Ruthlessness and clarity of object characterised the government's handling of the Republican problem. Among the remarkable features of the pro-treaty leadership from 1922 to 1925 were its grasp of the implications of the decision to settle for dominion status, the absence of *arrière pensée* and the refusal to negotiate with their opponents. The sole exception was the Collins-de Valera election pact of 1922, and even this bought time for the Provisional Government. Undoubtedly, the Republicans relied upon the government's reluctance to coerce old comrades; undoubtedly the government's success was largely due to suppressing this sentiment – if it was felt at all. In other fields, too, the new government pursued traditional British policy, but with an authority, a degree of public approbation and a single-mindedness which Irish administrations had lacked almost since the Act of Union. A second remarkable feature of the pro-treaty leadership in its early years was its collective executive ability. True, many of its members had forced themselves upward by sheer capacity in the hard school of the resistance movement; true also, they inherited professional civil servants – some repatriated from Great Britain – of the highest quality. None the less, if we compare their performance with other newcomers such as, say, the first Labour Government of 1924 in Britain, the sureness of decision and action manifested in Ireland seems extraordinary.

It was soon clear that the Irish Free State would enjoy efficient government, but whether she would enjoy democratic government was still an open question down to the eve of the Second World War. The original difficulty was that the major political parties had determined the issue which divided them not by electoral appeal but by the gun. The opposition refused to recognise the new state; and the new state in turn imprisoned – and in seventy-seven cases executed – its opponents as a measure of public safety. In 1924 Cosgrave's government began the long and difficult journey back to constitutionalism. It was a perilous undertaking. The harvest in 1924 was the worst since 1879; wage-cuts and reductions in the public service were the inevitable pre-Keynesian response to the growing European depression; and in the same year there was an army mutiny, primarily caused by demobilisation. Despite all this incendiary material ready for the spark, and despite the fact that the IRA had dumped and not surrendered their arms, Cosgrave and O'Higgins began to release the Republicans from prison in 1924; soon after, in March 1925, they took a decisive step in requiring a declaration of allegiance to the Irish Free State from all public servants and public bodies. This was not, as it might superficially appear, an act of discrimination against political opponents. Constitutional government was impossible unless the new state was accepted as a fact, and unless the traditional repudiation of authority was laid aside now that Irishmen would govern one another. The process of forcing the opposition on to a pacific and democratic course was under way.

It could scarcely have succeeded had de Valera proved intransigent in practice. But though his words and gestures seemed as defiant as ever, from the end of 1924 on he was conducting a masterly retreat from his former untenable position. First came the break with the IRA in November 1925, when that body (now popularly called 'the new IRA') determined to act as an exclusively military organisation, and to restore Irish unity by force of arms. Next, in March 1926, de Valera broke with the section of non-military Republicans who still refused to recognise the new state or to engage in political competition with the 'renegade' Cosgravites and other parliamentarians who accepted the treaty as a *fait accompli*. Two months later, de Valera set up a new party, Fianna Fail, and drew up a programme which not merely repeated the Republican orthodoxies, but also proposed some new departures, among them, protectionist legislation to encourage Irish industry, and the withholding of the annual payments now made to Great Britain for former land purchases and pensions. The next general election, held in June 1927, amply justified his return to parliamentary politics: Fianna Fail came within three seats of Cosgrave's party, which fell far short, moreover, of an absolute majority in the Dail.

De Valera had still one more pit of his own digging to climb out of: he had always refused to take the Oath of Allegiance required by the treaty of all members of the Dail before they could take their seats; and even now his party was debarred, by its self-denying ordinance, from acting in Parliament. Cosgrave provided the means of release, by introducing a Bill to render vacant the seats of all deputies who failed to take the Oath. This crisis enabled de Valera to carry his own sea-green incorruptibles with him, when swearing that he did not swear, and arguing that he signed the Oath 'in the same way that I would sign an autograph in a newspaper' – a clarification which scarcely clarified – he led his followers into the Chamber on 10 August 1927. Parliamentary government in Ireland had lived through its sickly infancy.

Once again, it would be wrong to assume that in proposing the Electoral Amendment Bill Cosgrave sought an immediate party advantage over his opponents. The government was well aware of the likely outcome, and of the possibility, or even probability, that Fianna Fail would come to power immediately with Labour support. It was not that they did not hate their political enemies. They did, with the depth of hatred that only a civil war can sink in men. But they loved liberal democracy even more. Nor had they a monopoly of this virtue. De Valera, hating no less, performed the equivalent services for his opponents in 1932–6. It was a fine thing, in the midst of much that was far from fine, that Cosgrave and de Valera, the major protagonists in the civil cold war from 1923 on, should ultimately have chosen constitutionalism, often against their immediate advantage, in every crisis. Great Britain had, after all, preached better than she knew under the Act of Union – and certainly preached better than she had practised.

The second great crisis for democracy in the new state coincided with the world depression of 1929–32. Cosgrave was still in power – the favourable result of a second general election in 1927 having enabled him to retain office with the support of the Farmers' Party. By 1931 the IRA had returned to the forefront, with illegal drillings, shootings and intimidation almost daily occurrences. Moreover, the organisation had now a left wing, Saor Eire, a quasi-Marxist group.

By 1931, besides, agricultural prices had fallen and unemployment had risen by 50 per cent since 1927; and once again the government reacted conventionally by imposing or endorsing wage-cuts, and reducing the level of public expenditure. With mounting threats of social disturbance and resurgent militarism, Cosgrave forced through a Public Safety Act along the lines, or even beyond the limits, of the once-familiar British coercion measures. Military courts with power to inflict the death penalty were set up to eradicate subversion; the cabinet was empowered to proclaim organisations dangerous to the state; and cat-and-mouse detentions of IRA suspects were legalised. Majority rule was vindicated; but to de Valera's and not Cosgrave's benefit. At the general election of February 1932, four months after the Public Safety Act had come into operation, Fianna Fail gained seventy-two seats, five short of an absolute majority, but sufficient to place de Valera in power – at last.

He had played his hand superbly. Having outmanœuvred the non-militant Republicans who had broken with him in 1926, he had proceeded to identify the two major groups of malcontents with his party, without subordinating the party to either. Promises of larger and more comprehensive doles, of protection and industrialisation, coupled with repudiation of the British debts, constituted a nice amalgam of nationalism and democracy. They clinched the wide and durable support which Fianna Fail enjoyed among the poorer classes, especially in the ranks of the small farmers and agricultural labourers; it was strong enough to survive innumerable economic disappointments in the 1930s. The Republican extremists were similarly ensnared. Fianna Fail opposed the Public Safety Bill bitterly in the Dail, and promised to disband the military courts if they were returned to power. The abolition of the Oath of Allegiance, of the governor-generalship, and of any other trappings of the British connection which proved vulnerable was, of course, an old plank in de Valera's platform on which Republicans of every degree of intensity could agree with conscience clear. De Valera further indicated that, once in office, he would release the political prisoners; and the IRA generally believed that this would be accompanied by wholesale dismissals of the 'traitors' who currently oppressed them from the ranks of the police, judiciary, army and public service. With all these attractions on display, Fianna Fail secured the support of the militarists both at the polls and, more important perhaps, to intimidate their opponents at election meetings. De Valera's attainment of office, confirmed in the following year when he sought and received an overall parliamentary majority, ended the second crisis for Irish democracy. The principle of responsible opposition had been vindicated, and the forces of potential violence were marshalled behind the parliamentary victors. De Valera's achievement was strongly reminiscent of Parnell's brilliant campaign of 1879–81. If any twentieth-century Irishman deserved to wear Parnell's mantle, it was the second 'Chief'.

Democracy in the Irish Free State entered its final phase of danger almost as soon as the second ended. The threat this time was that some form or other of totalitarianism would take root. The original spur toward this development (apart, of course, from current Continental example) lay in the expectation that the change in government in 1932 would also involve a change in the character of the state, with former office-holders more or less proscribed and persecuted for their earlier 'treason' to the Republic. On the one hand, some anticipated that the Cosgravites would not surrender power peacefully to their enemies. On the other, the IRA demanded a complete purge of the 'pro-treaty' civil servants, judges and army officers, and attempted to silence all anti- or un-Republican politicians: 'while we have fists, hands and boots to use, and guns if necessary, we will not allow free speech to traitors,'[1] declared its leader. The IRA practised what it preached: Cosgravite deputies were attacked, and Cosgravite meetings broken up by force. The threat of a *coup d'état* in reverse soon vanished. Men such as Cosgrave and Richard Mulcahy did not countenance a defiance of the electorate. But the danger that the gun would return to Irish politics increased. It was an escalatory process. The Cosgrave government's stern reaction in 1931 to the recrudescence of violence bred further violence directed against itself; in turn, the Cosgravites began to take up arms, originally in self-protection. De Valera's riposte, in July 1933, of establishing an armed police and seizing firearms, frightened his political opponents still more; and fears of their defencelessness led them farther along the road to force.

In 1933–4 each of the major parties in the Free State was threatened by the armed faction which supported it. The treatyites stood in the greater peril. In September 1933, after a second electoral defeat, they merged with two other groups, the small parliamentary Centre Party, and a new militant body of the right, the National Guard (earlier the Army Comrades Association), which had been formed in 1932, ostensibly to counter IRA violence at the elections. The amalgamation, called Fine Gael, had therefore an extra-parliamentary element; and more sinister still, it was the leader of this element, General Eoin O'Duffy, who became its first chairman. O'Duffy had recently been dismissed from the command of the police force by de Valera; and perhaps it seemed apt to the Cosgravites that he should now attempt to defend them from the other side of the fence. But there was soon some reason to fear that they had

aided the rise of the Irish Mussolini. O'Duffy clad his National Guard
in blue shirts and set them to drilling and other quasi-military
training, according to a pattern long familiar in the prehistory of
Irish revolutions. Had the arch-constitutionalists, after all, taken
aboard an embryo dictator? In reality, O'Duffy had, probably,
neither the desire nor the capacity to seize power; but after six years
of intensifying violence and political hatred, Ireland was in no
condition to tolerate totalitarian posturing.

In the event, O'Duffy proved to be but a Boulanger. De Valera
responded to the Blueshirts in 1934 precisely as Cosgrave had
responded to IRA extravagances in 1931: he revived the Public
Safety Act. Under its provisions, he banned a projected Blueshirt
march on Government Buildings in August 1934, and declared the
National Guard a prohibited body. When O'Duffy submitted
peacefully to these decrees, the worst was over. Almost immediately
afterward, Fine Gael seized a chance to rid the party of its embarrassing protector. When he sought party endorsement for a proposal
to withhold the land annuities not merely from the British, but also
from the Fianna Fail government, he was ejected from the chairman-
ship and also lost control of the erstwhile National Guard. The old
constitutionalists had decided not to cross the Rubicon into the land
of lawlessness. They returned, doubtless chastened and relieved, to
mere parliamentary opposition. The Blueshirt movement did not die
immediately: IRA reprisals and involvement in a species of land war
(non-payment of annuities and rates) in several areas kept it fitfully
alive. But after the autumn of 1934 it ceased to be, in any sense, a
national danger; and gradually, sloughed off by the parliamentarians,
it withered in isolation.

Ireland's equivalent of the 'left', the IRA, presented equal difficulties to Fianna Fail, but de Valera proved as skilled in office as he
had been when out of power. He offered no direct assault for several
years. On the contrary, he moved immediately as far towards
Republican symbolism as a constitutional minister safely could,
without a downright repudiation of the treaty. This enabled him to
blur, in the popular mind, the distinction between Fianna Fail
and the extremists. Meanwhile, the latter, even if carelessly and
half-contemptuously, blessed this work as constituting a modest contribution towards their objective. Concurrently, de Valera concentrated all political attentions upon his struggle with the forces of the
'right'. Again, what seemed to be a common cause kept the government and the IRA in an informal alliance down to the end of 1934.
When de Valera disarmed the treatyites, armed a section of the
police and set up a special police division recruited from hardened
Republicans to suppress the Blueshirts, the IRA could only support

him warmly. But there was another side to the medal – which they saw too late. De Valera redeemed his election promises at once in 1932 by releasing the IRA prisoners and repealing the Public Safety Act. But he did not fulfil the IRA expectation that the police, army, judiciary and civil service would be purged of treatyites. A handful – O'Duffy among them – were thrown to the Republican wolves. But de Valera resisted the temptation – perhaps, as a lover of the rule of law, he felt none – to introduce a spoils system in the Irish state. Moreover, he stopped short of any really dangerous assault upon the treaty. The Statute of Westminster in 1931 had rendered it constitutionally safe to remove the Oath of Allegiance. But, the governor-generalship being a more doubtful issue, he contented himself with pseudo-revolutionary expressions of contempt in this particular case.

Most important of all was the fact that each of de Valera's measures against the National Guard could be turned with equal force against the extreme Republicans when he saw fit to do so. The revived Public Safety Act, the special police and the ban on firearms were as appropriate a counter to violence on the left as to violence on the right. Moreover, quite apart from the machinery of repression, the long campaign against the Blueshirts had conditioned (or reconditioned) Irish public opinion to the view that the state must assert its sovereignty, come what might, and that it alone had the right to assemble and deploy armed force. In short, the IRA had been outflanked on both sides. The government's tone and measures were sufficiently Republican to leave only the radical fringe seriously dissatisfied with their inadequacy, while its firmness had established unassailably the authority of Parliament. From 1932 onward the IRA was sinking, in the popular estimation, from a powerful body of armed idealists on whose sufferance the government was allowed to govern to a divided body whose only common principles appeared to be an unattainable political idea and an ineradicable faith in violence. Under pressure, the extremists began to break up in 1935, through differences over tactics, priorities and the validity of socialist values. Simultaneously, a few brutal and wanton killings by the IRA (none of them, incidentally, sanctioned by the leadership) produced a final national revulsion against the organisation. De Valera, who had used the military tribunals cautiously in 1935 to draw the teeth of the extremists, decided in June 1936 that the day of reckoning had come at last. The IRA was proscribed as an illegal body; its chief of staff was imprisoned; and its public assemblies came to an end. The third crisis of parliamentarianism was over.

De Valera had established a political ascendancy over all which was to last with brief interruptions for almost a quarter of a century. Not only were the forces of violence in disarray, but Fine Gael and

Labour had also been gravely weakened by their own errors of judgement, by Fianna Fail's successful handling of the working (and especially the rural working) classes, and above all by de Valera's ever-increasing stature, as political strategist and popular hero alike. Already he had passed the mysterious limit which, in Ireland at least, divides the 'uncrowned kings' from the remainder; alone among modern Irishmen he had reached the rank of O'Connell, Parnell and – if the anti-kings be counted also – Carson. Well for his countrymen that he was, ultimately speaking, selfless and democratic. But as he played his hand from 1932 to 1936, it needed responsive selflessness and democracy from his countrymen, not least from his principal political opponents, for him to win all the tricks. Despite the Blueshirt imbroglio, and the apparent threats to their persons, the Cosgravites held in the end to constitutionalism; and like Cosgrave and de Valera, the mass of the Irish people had been too long pupils in the school of English liberalism to countenance political philosophies of might.

The IRA might ask, had the Easter Rising more popular support at first than we have now? The answer was that 1916 belonged already to a vanished world. No longer could men rise in Ireland against British domination and its symbols; no longer could they glorify blood-sacrifices, in Pearsean fashion, without knowing, too, the agonies and squalor which were their companions; no longer could they preach the rule of the gun without drifting sooner or later toward the totalitarians. Nor were the majority of the members of either the National Guard or the militant Republicans exempt from the underlying Irish instinct for constitutional processes. There were few, perhaps no, fascists or communists in the full Continental senses of the terms amongst the Irish protagonists. At least, the original causes of division – civil war animosities, personal fear and vengeance and rarefied abstract goals – were more significant in almost every case than the clothes borrowed from exotic ideologies to dress up in on the way to war.

Meanwhile, the event which occasioned the civil war, the treaty, dominated Ireland's external relations no less than its domestic conflicts down to 1939. In one area, separation went steadily from strength to strength. Griffith and Collins were vindicated in their argument that the agreement of 1921 set no bounds to the march of the nation. First, the Cosgrave government pressed for international acceptance as a full sovereign state. In 1923 the Irish Free State entered the League of Nations, and in the next year appointed its own minister in Washington, a step which no other dominion had yet taken. This was followed in 1926 by a bid for election to the League Council, which, although unsuccessful immediately, led to the enunciation of the principle that dominions were full equals of Great Britain in the international community. In turn this paved the way for the resolution, partly due to the pressure of the Irish delegates, at the Imperial Conference of 1926, that all states within the British Empire were 'equal in status, in no way subordinate to one another in any aspect of their domestic or external affairs'. Thus, within five years, and despite the desperate struggle to establish the supremacy of the new Irish government on its own soil, the remaining traces of British hegemony had been removed, and 'dominion status' radically redefined. These advances were confirmed and clarified at the next Imperial Conference in 1930; and pressures generated then – again partly through Irish agitation – ended in the Statute of Westminster in 1931, empowering any dominion to repeal, uni-laterally, United Kingdom legislation hitherto binding in its territory. The way was now clear for a repudiation by the Irish Free State of any distasteful clause in the treaty: in fact, in the Commons debate on the measure in November 1931, Churchill resisted it upon precisely this ground.

Meanwhile, the Free State had already struck a blow at the imperial structure in another vulnerable region in 1929. In accepting the ultimate jurisdiction of the Permanent Court of International Justice to determine disputes between signatory states, it repudiated the imperial principle that disputes between the United Kingdom and the dominions, or between one dominion and another, were domestic matters, not subject to international adjudication. What is especially noteworthy in all this is that the constitutional revolution was essentially the work of the treatyite government. De Valera was to harvest the separatist crop in the 1930s, but it was his opponents who had sown the seed. It was they – ironically enough – who had established that membership of the empire was essentially voluntary, that it derogated in no way from independent international status, and that it bound the dominions to common action only to the degree to which they were prepared to bind themselves. It was Cosgrave's government also which laid the foundations of an independent foreign policy. This was quite disassociated from specific British interests, being in part neutralist and in part an expression of the small state's concern for international order in a world where powers and power-blocs sought their own advantages. The models, if any, were Switzerland and Sweden.

De Valera, then, found the ball teed for him when he entered office in 1932. He felt, to say the least, no moral obligation to preserve the treaty; and Cosgrave had prepared the way for its amendment. De Valera soon removed the Oath of Allegiance to the Crown, appeals to the Privy Council from Irish judicial decisions and

British citizenship for Irish subjects. The British government protested that each of these repeals violated the solemn constitutional concordat of 1922. De Valera was unmoved. On the one hand, he pleaded the invalidity of the treaty; on the other, he could rely upon the Statute of Westminster which had undermined the British case. These early triumphs were followed by a coup in 1936, when the abdication of Edward VIII suddenly presented the Irish government with the initiative. They proceeded to delete the king (and his alter ego, the governor-general) from the constitution, and to employ him for Irish purposes solely in the role in which de Valera had originally cast him in his External Association proposal of 1921. Henceforward, the Crown merely represented the Irish Free State in international business, and even then only whenever the Free State was acting in concert with the other members of the empire. This was followed up by a new Irish constitution in 1937 – again unilaterally adopted. In terms of Anglo-Irish relations, the two new turns of the screw were a provision for a president, as head of state, and a change in title from Irish Free State to Ireland (or, in Gaelic, Eire). None of this apparent brinkmanship in the 1930s was really dangerous. The basic weakness of the British position was the fixed resolve that Ireland must never leave the empire. So long as the Irish stopped short of a direct and specific repudiation of all imperial connections, the British government would in the end find a formula to reconcile virtually any Irish innovation with its own theories of sovereignty. There was irony, bordering upon farce, in the manner in which the captive in the imperial tower dismantled so many of the confining walls that the gaoler scarcely knew what he had left.

Great Britain was also routed on the other front which the Cosgrave government had opened up. De Valera was elected president of the Council of the League of Nations (to which Ireland had eventually won admittance in 1930) in the same year as he came to power at home. At once, he carried forward the standard of an independent Irish foreign policy. It was not that he opposed all, or even most, of the proposals which the British government endorsed. In fact, he joined the Free State with Great Britain in advocating the admission of the Soviet Union to the League, the application of sanctions against Italy in 1935 and non-intervention (as well as non-recognition of Franco) in Spain. But his basic purpose was the repudiation of force as the arbiter of international politics; and in the name of small nations, he did not spare the great powers in his addresses. It is equally noteworthy, perhaps, that Irish foreign policy paid as little heed to conservative clerical opinion at home as to British interests: de Valera's stands on the Russian, Italian and Spanish issues of the 1930s speak for themselves.

So far the Irish manipulation of the treaty to enlarge the independent standing of the Free State had been a series of costless victories. But another issue taken up by de Valera on his advent to office in 1932 was not so easy. This was his repudiation of the financial agreement of 1926 between Great Britain and the Irish Free State, which had laid down the annual payments due to the British government for earlier land purchase advances, loans to Irish local authorities and pensions to former British administrators. The United Kingdom at once attempted to recover these monies by imposing additional duties on imports from Ireland; and the Irish government responded in kind. It was nearly six years before this mutually injurious tariff war concluded. Meanwhile Irish imports fell by one-half, and Irish exports by three-fifths. The ultimate bargain struck between de Valera and Chamberlain in the London agreement which ended this economic conflict in 1938 was, in narrow financial terms, most favourable to the Irish: £10 million was accepted by Great Britain as 'a final settlement' of all questions of Irish indebtedness for past credits and services. There were, moreover, certain psychological satisfactions: another struggle had been 'won' – at least on points – and another door closed for ever on Ireland's experiences under the Act of Union. But the hidden costs were also very large. Men live not in the long run but in the present; and some at least of the terrible poverty of the Irish masses in the 1930s was attributable to the pursuit of national *amour propre* of a particularly dubious variety. Worse still, another term of noise and fury had been added to all the years already spent in sterile political retrospection.

One by-product of the London agreement was much more significant than the main *rapprochement*. The British government surrendered its Irish naval bases. 'It was', writes Mr Coogan, 'possibly the only successful application of Chamberlain's appeasement policy.' Perhaps Chamberlain considered that good relations with Ireland in a European war, which was already probable, were worth the price. If so, he may well have paid too much. Not merely neutrality, but 'pro-British neutrality' would very likely have been the Irish attitude, whatever the fate of the naval bases. On the other hand, British possession of the bases during the war might have made Irish neutrality impracticable, and forced Ireland sooner or later into the Allied camp. At any rate, Great Britain's magnanimity, folly or recognition of natural justice (as one wishes) completed by 1938 the process of constitutional liberation, except in that limited and shadowy region where it seemed to Ireland's advantage to call a halt.

Constitutional liberation, yes – but, as every full-blooded nationalist of the day would have said, for only twenty-six of the Irish counties. The Boundary Commission failed to salvage anything from the wreck of 'Irish unity' in 1921. First the Irish civil war postponed the application for its institution; next, the Northern Ireland government refused to appoint a member – and, by implication, to recognise that its current boundaries were negotiable. Then the law contributed its customary measure of delay before the British government was authorised to name a member on behalf of Northern Ireland. Altogether, two unnecessary years elapsed before the Commission's deliberations opened, and this time told steadily against the Free State, as vested interests developed in the 'border' and the 'viability' of the severed fragment of the island became apparent.

The adjudicators came to the matter with three distinct and conflicting purposes. MacNeill, the Free State representative, expected the cession of all areas reasonably contiguous to the border which contained substantial Nationalist majorities – more than one-third of the land area of the six counties. Fisher, the Ulsterman, wanted a frontier band of solid Unionist districts, without regard to the size of the nationalist areas behind the *cordon sanitaire*. This would have meant an 'Ulster' no smaller in area, if different in territorial composition. Feetham, the chairman, once a member of Milner's 'kindergarten' in South Africa, was also a judge, and lawyer-like, crabbed in statutory interpretation and respectful of visible institutions. Not merely had the treaty failed to specify that large transfers of territory were in contemplation; two of the leading negotiators, Chamberlain and Lord Birkenhead, their memories now conveniently short, publicly indicated that only trivial rectifications had been intended. These interventions must have reinforced Feetham's penchant for the existing frontier. Meanwhile, MacNeill, again the evil genius (or, perhaps, the Don Quixote) of Irish separatism, helped on the destruction of nationalist hopes by remaining in the Commission until the eleventh hour, keeping his government in ignorance of the trend of its deliberations, and then resigning precipitately when a report advocating only minor changes – and those as much at the expense of the south as of the north – was on the point of publication. Cosgrave, in despair, settled for the existing boundary as a permanent arrangement in a hastily concluded post-treaty treaty in December 1925. 'Northern Ireland' was safe at last. But had the Boundary Commission represented a peril at all to the north in 1925? Even had its findings been all that Griffith and Collins had expected, could they have been enforced after almost five years of independent constitutional government in the six counties? Theoretically, British legislation – in fact the existing legislation – was enough to effect the transfer. But past experience was not encouraging on this head, and the north-eastern counties were in an incomparably stronger situation in 1925 than in 1914. It is difficult not to believe that Protestant Ulster, having prudently repudiated the Commission in advance, would yet again have found a way around statutes and parliamentary majorities, whatever happened.

'War changes everything,' said Thucydides; but this was far from apparent in Eire between 1939 and 1945. Instead, the conflict seemed to sustain the status quo for perhaps a decade. De Valera had prepared carefully for the Armageddon. As president of the League of Nations in 1938, he became painfully certain of the coming devastation, and was quick to declare his neutrality in advance. But, having rendered neutrality practicable by securing in 1938 the Irish naval bases hitherto in British hands, he also made it clear that Eire would serve British interests to any reasonable limit, short of war. Three months before the invasion of Poland, he assured Great Britain that Irish territory would never be used for hostile actions. As he had further (if tacitly) promised, Eire's neutrality was in fact one-sided. The German forces, economy, and propaganda and espionage apparatus did not enjoy the advantages and opportunities which de Valera afforded their British counterparts from first to last. Germany quietly accepted this 'special relationship'. Presumably she considered (as presumably de Valera had calculated she would) that the denial of the use of the Irish Atlantic ports to Great Britain constituted a sufficient compensation.

At any rate, Eire, unscathed, contributed heavily to the war effort of her hereditary foe. Directly, Great Britain was supported by 30,000 Irish recruits in her armed services, and by a very much larger number of Irish men and women in her work force; by food supplied; and by mounting unspent sterling balances. Indirectly, the Irish neutrality laws, as they were actually applied, worked decidedly in favour of Great Britain. For example, no British airmen forced to land in Eire were ever interned there – only Germans. It was, of course, natural that the British government, especially in the phases following the fall of France and preceding the invasion of 1944, should have been tempted to end some of its difficulties by seizing Eire by force of arms. After all, the price for their exclusion from the western and southern ports was very high; there must have been many moments when the London Agreement seemed wanton folly. Churchill, who succeeded Chamberlain as prime minister in 1940, had himself fought fiercely in the negotiations of 1921 precisely to prevent the present embarrassment; and perhaps most powerful of all in raising the temptation to invade was the fact that the British people had been habituated for four hundred years to regard the whole of Ireland as their natural base. But once again de Valera had calculated nicely. The balance of advantage, even for Great Britain, lay in amicable relations between the islands. In fact, there are some indications that it was British influence which saved Eire from armed invasion by the United States in 1943 or 1944 – even if the Americans intended no more than a shotgun marriage, if that would suffice. Great Britain had had incomparable and mortifying experience in casting Irish equations. She had learnt from this that immediate gains might prove in the long run too expensive.

Doubtless, it was much to survive intact in 1939–45. But the domestic costs of neutrality were not inconsiderable. Essentially, the war promoted what was by now a *quieta non movere* state of politics and society. The condition reached in the political system by the mid-1930s was simply perpetuated. The two main parties, deriving from the treaty division, engrossed 70 to 80 per cent of the parliamentary representation, with Fianna Fail close to – on occasion actually attaining – an absolute majority in the Dail. Most of the remaining seats were shared by the sectional parties of labour and agriculture, with independents and ephemeral extremist groups accounting for the balance. By 1939 Fianna Fail seemed, temporarily at least, to have exhausted its creative purposes. The new democratic and constitutional systems had been established; Republican symbolism had been imposed up to the level which de Valera considered prudent in the light of other national interests; the very modest measures of social reform which were consequential on the economic war and the party's dependence upon workers' and small farmers' votes had been carried through with a decided air of finality; and the limitations of protectionist industrialism of the old Sinn Fein variety had been thoroughly exposed. But the extinct volcanoes of 1939 were not to be disturbed for nine years more.

It is a speculation, but it seems a fair one, to attribute to the circumstances of the war this protracted retention of office after Fianna Fail's positive programme had petered out and the government's functions become increasingly executive. De Valera reigned as the man 'who keeps us out of the war', the tortuous but triumphant statesman, the tamer of violent Republicans – how dangerous to disturb his power upon the very brink of the abyss. However sound the general proposition, an important side-effect was an intensification of the national acquiescence in immobility. Moreover, in the Second World War, unlike the First, the check on emigration to North America had no significant effect upon Irish political or social development. That emigration was already small; and on this occasion the British factories and service industries possessed an insatiable appetite for Irish labour. Thus potential discontents dispersed while fears of change remained specific. Meanwhile the bleakness and meanness of material life in wartime – even in an island of peace – were matched by emotional and intellectual impoverishment. In a society already small, inward-looking and self-absorbed, the general, compulsory and unheroic isolation reinforced all that was static or retrogressive in its composition. It was not easy to recover from these deprivations.

The spell was half broken at the general election of 1948, when Fianna Fail, weighed down by maladministration, the euphoria bred by sixteen years of power, and the onset of postwar depression, was driven out of office. But the Irish political system was by now – as it still remains – extraordinarily rigid. Fianna Fail's 'defeat' left them with 46 per cent of the Dail seats; and their several opponents could replace them only by sinking their own grievous quarrels and acting collectively. The new combination was a rainbow spread of every colour in the Irish political spectrum, from the most to the least conservative forces in the land, whether we take social, economic, religious or nationalistic factors as the criterion. The leadership and the lion's share of the ministries in the Coalition Government of 1948–51 fell to the old treatyite party, now Fine Gael. But this did not mean an absolute control of policy. 'Coalitions', Jennings has pointed out, 'are *necessarily* unprincipled.' All elements may be essential in such a government; and even the smallest can impose its will upon the rest, given recklessness and favourable conditions.

The group which gained most relative to its numbers in the Coalition was a small new party, a mere ten strong, led by the son of Maud Gonne, Sean MacBride, long a hero of the violent Republicans. The party was itself a coalition of several types of Irish 'radical', Republican and socialistic, austere and demagogic. At first sight – and this was almost all the Irish electorate had had of them in 1948 – MacBride and his lieutenant, Noel Browne, seemed, just possibly, the heralds of a second revolution. Their first success in manipulating the cabinet which they had joined gave some colour to this impression. In the spring of 1949, a Republic of Ireland Act swept the twenty-six counties out of the Commonwealth. This bewildering measure had placed the old treatyites – numerically dominant in the new government – at the head of the Republican column, dragging the chagrined but helpless de Valera and his party in their train! Not since the repeal of the corn laws, or perhaps Disraeli's handling of the second Reform Bill, was so bizarre a political spectacle witnessed in the British Isles. The British counterpart of the Irish statute, the Ireland Act of 1949, happily left the new Republic all the advantages of the old relationship. Whatever the forms, the Irish were still in British eyes a 'non-foreign' people, to be dealt with by the Commonwealth Relations Office, and invested in Great Britain with the same rights and obligations as citizens of the United Kingdom. As in 1939–45, the British government did not allow racial resentment or old habits of thought to over-ride their judgement of the balance of advantage. But the Ireland Act had also to reassure the northern Unionists. It guaranteed that Northern Ireland should never leave the United Kingdom unless she did so voluntarily and on her own initiative. The formal, final surrender by the imperial parliament of its theoretical right to dispose of north-eastern Ireland was important. It seemed to close the last (if very unpromising) avenue of hope for the constitutional nationalists.

Ireland, Balfour once wrote, taught him in the end 'how much more important in the eyes of ordinary men are *nominal* differences than real ones'. If the declaration of a Republic can be justified, it is on this ground. Any formal connection with Great Britain was felt by most Irishmen to be *pro tanto* a diminution of the free and equal status which they claimed. To this extent, the observation that the Republic of Ireland Act was tragically precipitate because India was soon to show that republican forms were compatible with Commonwealth associations is beside the point. Proximity, cultural and geographical alike, and the peculiar historical relationship between the two islands, meant that in the Irish case even the most shadowy connection seemed to imply some residue of subordination. The real question is not whether anything at all was gained, but whether the psychological satisfactions were bought too dearly. The satisfactions were genuine but trivial; only the tenderest of Republican consciences could have felt much burdened by the pathetic remnants of the imperial tie which had survived de Valera's depredations.

One ostensible object of the *volte face* of Fine Gael was the demobilisation of the armed Republicans; now that a Republic had been reached at last, perhaps they would quietly disband. But the early 1950s saw a marked revival in the fortunes and activities of the IRA, partly because such a movement springs, to some extent, from forces independent of its objective, and partly because *Hibernia irredenta* still left them with a world to conquer. It may be noted, in passing, that the second and more recent revival seems essentially different in character. If the IRA is busy and intrusive again today in southern Ireland, it is as a derivative of an independently generated northern movement. Republicanism in the Republic is now strongly reminiscent of militant Irish-Americanism in the United States in the closing decades of the nineteenth century and performs roughly equivalent political and other supportive functions.

A graver loss of the Republic of Ireland Act may have been the prospect, however unhopeful immediately, of reaching an accommodation with the north. To Protestant Ulster, some association with the British Crown was the one eternal and indispensable guarantee. It was doubtless with Irish unity in view that de Valera, almost from the outset of his political career, had striven to distinguish those symbols of British authority which did not derogate from Irish independence from those which did. Now wanton boys had torn away his delicate constitutional construction. As if this were not enough, the Coalition Government embarked concurrently (1949–50) upon a vulgar, futile and, in many cases, disingenuous 'anti-partition campaign'. This consisted in bloody-shirt waving, the collection of large sums of money for the support of Ulster Republicans, the manufacture of propaganda and innumerable tedious hours at the new Council of Europe, which the Irish delegates treated as a species of forum for the elaboration of their country's wrongs. Given the temper and preoccupations of postwar Europe, and the new constitutional bulwarks of the Northern Ireland parliament, it would have been difficult to devise a line of conduct less likely to achieve the professed object of the government, namely, to draw back the six lost counties to the Irish fold.

MacBride having dealt with the past, Browne attempted to hurry on the future, and in doing so he destroyed the Coalition. The Health Bill of 1950, for which he was responsible, set out to provide free state pediatric and maternity services. It hardly needs saying that the medical profession constituted an implacable opponent. But in Ireland it proved unnecessary for the doctors to exert themselves politically in the familiar fashion. The Catholic hierarchy opposed the scheme upon the grounds, first, that it interfered with individual and family rights, secondly, that it represented a dangerous intrusion by the state into personal life, and thirdly, that it might open a door to contraception or even abortion. It is noteworthy, however, that the opinion of the bishops had been sought, not proffered, and that the hierarchy made no attempt to embarrass the government or arouse the public. The politicians, Browne included, were in no small part to blame for the subsequent imbroglio, which revealed almost ludicrous misunderstandings at certain stages in the affair. Browne himself was eventually abandoned by his leader MacBride, and repudiated by the remainder of the cabinet. He had a sweet but profitless revenge when, in May 1951, he played the leading part in bringing down the Coalition Government, and replacing them by yet another Fianna Fail administration. Although it happened 'only yesterday', the episode already seems what an earlier generation might have called 'gothick'. It belongs in spirit, not to the world of *aggiornamento*, but to the family of clerical-political confusions which bedevilled nineteenth-century Irish public life on the issues of education, property rights, resistance to lawful authority and the rest. In another aspect, it illustrates the pitiful condition of alternative government in Ireland, where the necessity for all opposition factions to amalgamate blindly if Fianna Fail were to be replaced produced cabinets prone to intermittent bouts of recklessness and cowardice.

The political pattern of the immediate postwar years was repeated in the 1950s. When de Valera's second administration fell in 1954, it was replaced by a second Coalition Government. This was in turn succeeded by de Valera's third ministry in 1957. In his last year of office, 1959, on his way to the pantheon of the presidency, de Valera attempted to break the constrictions which proportional representation had placed upon the political system. The single, non-transferable voting which he now proposed would unquestionably have favoured the major parties, and in particular his own. It would have produced on most occasions impregnable majorities in the Dail. But Fianna Fail's self-interest was so obviously being served by de Valera's measure that the majority of the electors, who for one reason or another opposed his party, rejected it in a national referendum. The consequence was, and is, a continuation of the state of near-equality in parliamentary representation between Fianna Fail and its combined opponents. From 1957 to 1972 the latter were never sufficiently concerted to form a third administration. But neither has Fianna Fail enjoyed a clear majority for long.

The second Coalition (1954–7) had, however, its points of interest. Its downfall, like that of the first, was the work of MacBride-ites. On this occasion it was MacBride's own motion deploring the lack of an activist policy toward partition which proved fatal. But in the interval, like the first breath of spring, came faint indications that the end of sterile politics was close at hand. One harbinger was the dignity and circumspection manifested by the Irish delegates newly admitted to the United Nations in 1956, a joyous contrast to the behaviour of the first representatives at the Council of Europe seven years before. But while it was much to behave fitly as citizens of the world, it was a great deal more to attempt to wrest the economy at home from the slow decline in which it had seemed fixed since 1945, if not in fact from the very inauguration of the new state; and this is what the second Coalition showed signs of doing in its later days. The establishment of an Industrial Development Authority and the first moves toward national economic planning undertaken by the Coalition Government marked the commencement of a new age. Not until de Valera, the very epitome of abstract anglocentric politics, quitted the stage in 1959, was this fully apparent. But from the outset of the 1960s the Republic was increasingly absorbed in contemporary concerns; 1916, the treaty, the fratricide seemed dying issues. Perhaps they would rise again only as history, and no longer as daily torments. Perhaps Griffith's terrible questions in the treaty debates, 'Is there to be no living Irish nation? Is the Irish nation to be the dead past or the prophetic future?' would not need to be asked again.

But it is one thing to lay ghosts at home; another, to prevent their emigration. One can still be haunted from across a border; and, no more than the British rhetoric and stances of centuries, do the rhetoric and stances of the south for fifty years cease to bear bitter fruit because they have withered where first they flowered.

6

The New Economy

'We are the most conservative revolutionaries in history,' said the most radical of the new ministers, Kevin O'Higgins, after the formation of the Irish Free State. O'Higgins might have excepted the Dutch and the Americans, but in general he was right. Religion may be one explanation of the restraint. The establishment of peasant proprietorship was undoubtedly another. By the time that independence was achieved the number of the very smallest farms – less than 30 acres – had fallen from 200,000 to 100,000 over the preceding thirty years. But 100,000 still represented one-third of all Irish holdings. Moreover, the vast majority of the remaining farms were in the 30–50 acre category. The title deeds had been changed but not the essential structure of agriculture. Like French small farmers – and for similar reasons – the new Irish owners combined extreme political radicalism, of a rather abstract kind, with social and economic immobility. This was due partly to historical experience; Irish farming had not been solely or even mainly a capitalistic activity under the Act of Union. Peasant proprietorship failed to alter this fundamentally. In some respects, it perpetuated unprofitable agriculture by rendering the former tenant absolute master of a very small holding. Generally, he had not the technical knowledge, the mechanical equipment or the money needed to wring a competence from such a place. Yet the system was tolerable because of another factor in the social pattern – the ease and prevalence of emigration for the farmer's dependants. *Mutatis mutandis*, all this applied equally to the towns and cities. Emigration was the enemy of economic change, the solvent of economic conflict. More than any other single force it was responsible for the immobility of Ireland – the politics of constitutional forms apart – in the opening decades of the present century.

This immobility was, in part at least, faithfully reflected in the new state. We should note initially that Ireland immediately after independence resembled Norway or Belgium at the same stage much more closely than it did the newly freed Australian or American colonies. It already possessed an elaborate infrastructure of public works and communications, of banks and other monetary instruments, of wholesale and retail outlets; skilled civil servants and a sophisticated administrative system; houses and hospitals, sufficient in quantity at least; universal primary education and literacy; and cheap, plentiful and relatively advanced secondary schools and universities. In all of these respects, it was already a developed country. In some indeed it seemed 'overdeveloped'. For example, the transport network was too complex and too costly for the traffic; the work force had to carry a relatively high proportion of very old and very young; far more professionally trained people were produced than the country could possibly absorb; and the commercial banks were too many, overcapitalised and uncompetitive. This face of the Irish economy represented stability almost to the point of stagnation. It also provided an ironic commentary on 'breaking the connection with England'. For after independence the Irish output of manpower, professional and unskilled alike, went, not decreasingly, but increasingly to Great Britain, while the Irish government and banks continued to pursue British fiscal and economic policies at a respectful distance, and the many Irish workers who belonged to British trade unions retained their memberships. In short, the Irish Free State, in this sphere, remained effectively a provincial segment of a mature economy in the British Isles.

It might appear, at first sight, that the other face of the new state resembled the 'newly emerging' nations of today. Its principal products and exports were primary commodities. Most of its population was rural. It imported the overwhelming majority of the manufactures which it consumed. Almost all its own industries were minute and relatively inefficient. The domestic market was extremely small, and in the appropriate geographical context, Europe and North America, its per capita income was very low. But the similarities to, say, Malaysia or Kenya today were in reality superficial. In the first place, the existing administrative, social and economic infrastructure meant that the demands upon national investment in this sphere were negligible immediately. Next we should recall that it was only by European and North American standards that per capita income was low; by the standards of the world generally it was very high. But perhaps the most striking difference arose from Ireland's total lack of natural resources and her proximity and ready access to great industrial and urban complexes. These rendered very acute the difficulties of establishing manufacture upon a significant scale, and even of retaining her work force substantially intact. Thus, the true character of the Free State under this second head was not so much that of an underdeveloped country, as that of a pocket of underdevelopment in an advanced region, such as the Maritime Provinces constitute in Canada as a whole or as Sicily does in Italy. It was, in Maoist terminology, neither town nor country, but a green fringe on the urban edge.

For almost the first forty years of the life of the new state, the response to this situation was feeble, and the economic benefits of political independence very small. Between 1921 and 1959 the Irish rate of economic growth was only 1 per cent per annum. In the same period the population declined almost continuously. Yet the country's external assets remained extraordinarily large in relation to the gross national product throughout all these years: they invariably approached or exceeded $1 billion in current values. The great majority of this money was invested in one form or another in Great Britain. Moreover, apart from one small loan in the 1920s, and some minor assistance after 1945 under Marshall Aid, Ireland never borrowed abroad, although she could certainly have done so on relatively favourable terms at most stages. In short, neither capital nor credit was used for development to any large extent before 1959. The bulk of national investment went toward the replacement or extension of the existing network of houses, roads, schools, hospitals and the like, and not into the directly productive sectors of the economy. It would, of course, be anachronistic to condemn the first ministries in the new state for their failure to adopt the policies, or evaluate their problems in the terms, which are fashionable today. Not merely did Gladstonianism still reign in treasury departments the world over; Irish independence arrived at a moment peculiarly inopportune for the economics of development. International trade was contracting, prices were falling and, as usual in these circumstances, the primary producers were worst hit of all. None the less, it cannot be emphasised too often that constitutional autonomy produced little significant change – indeed very few significant efforts to produce change – in the structure or behaviour of the Irish economy for more than three decades.

There were, of course, some attempts to strike new courses. The most ambitious and coherent came in the early years of the first de Valera regime, 1932–6. Alternative markets to the United Kingdom were sought for Irish agricultural exports, while protective tariffs were simultaneously set up to enable native industries to develop. Neither policy was successful, as might indeed have been predicted, for the government had been moved by political rather than economic considerations. First, the idea of national self-sufficiency, with the corollary of protection, had come to be accepted as a mark of doctrinal purity among Irish nationalists. This was Griffith's legacy, although the legatees proved to be his political enemies rather than his friends. More specifically, the economic war with Great Britain practically forced de Valera's government to attempt to develop new export markets and new manufacturing industries at home. Again, it was the worst of times for such adventures. But even had international circumstances been favourable, success was unlikely, for de Valera's experiments in the 1930s represented frontal assaults, at once crude and puny, upon a very powerful economic force – the long-established dependence of a hinterland upon a developed centre for its markets and supplies. Moreover, de Valera himself was as lacking in acquisitive and commercial instincts as in economic sophistication. His vision of Ireland free was a land of small farms, modest incomes and simple lives. 'The Ireland we dreamed of', he once said, 'would be the home of a people who valued material wealth only as the basis of a right living, of a people who were satisfied with a frugal comfort and devoted their leisure to the things of the spirit. It would, in a word, be the home of a people living the life that God desires men to live.' There was no room for economic miracles of the modern kind in this amalgam of monastic and physiocratic ideals, encased in a Celtic reliquary. Not all his lieutenants – and certainly not his eventual successor, Sean Lemass – saw the matter in quite these terms. But in the 1930s, and for many years thereafter, it was de Valera who called the tune in Fianna Fail.

But in one important area of economic life, the state corporation, the Irish Free State was almost from the beginning among the advanced nations of the world. Collectivist economic organisation – which some call socialism – was never a matter of doctrine or even of conscious deliberation in Ireland. It was largely a matter of necessity. Irish commercial and industrial activity was practically confined to family firms. With a few exceptions, the scale of operations was small, the practice conservative, and the goal limited to the retention of an existing market. Traditions of technical or managerial skill, or of investment in private enterprise, did not exist. Private capital would not or could not venture into commercial activity of any significance, where the number of joint-stock public companies was very small. This is the background which explains the importance of the state corporation in the Irish Free State. Such an intervention by central government had, of course, been foreshadowed in the nineteenth century, most significantly of all perhaps in the attempts of the Congested Districts Board to stimulate the transport, fishery, agricultural and similar industries in the poorest regions. But only after independence did the state enter unhesitatingly into the area conventionally ascribed to private activity.

Two innovations of the Cosgrave government may be used as illustrations of the new development. First, in the more likely field of public utilities, came the establishment of the Electricity Supply Board in 1927. Alongside the suppression of the private electricity companies, a new hydro-electric scheme for harnessing the Shannon waters was carried into effect by the state. Technically as well as politically, it was a daring venture in its day, and encountered corresponding opposition. But technically as well as politically, the innovators were ultimately justified. For the first time, Ireland was making a significant contribution toward the production of the power she used, and from the beginning the Board operated as efficiently as any private business would have done. Sugar is the second example of a product which the new state set out to supply from its own resources. Again the device of a semi-autonomous state board to supervise the establishment of the industry and to regulate its subsequent operations was employed. Again the state company was inevitably involved in 'ordinary' commerce – to say nothing of the education of primary producers. Again the experiment succeeded. The first sugar factory, established at Carlow by the Cosgrave government, was followed by three more set in other areas suitable for sugar beet in the late 1930s. Moreover, just as the Electricity Supply Board was led gradually into doing more than producing power – into planning rural electrification, into marketing electrical products, and into undertaking electrical installation and repairs – so too the Sugar Company diversified laterally into the manufacture of sugar products, and even into the processing of other foods and the production and marketing of prepared foods generally.

The pattern of economic development through the medium of the state corporation was repeated by Cosgrave's successors, until the number of such boards and companies had, by 1960, increased to almost fifty. It is a difficult matter to quantify, but it is probably fair to conclude that they then employed some 10 per cent of the Irish work force and were responsible for more than 5 per cent of the national product. Some of the corporations were essentially administrative in character, or involved in activities which private business everywhere eschews. But many others were extensions to new fields of the sort of productive undertaking of our two examples. In these cases, the corporation almost always originated either in the state stepping in where private business had failed – as was the case with steel production – or in the state supplying a need which private business had ignored – as was the case with machine-won peat, for fuel and power. Some general underlying purposes for these intrusions may be inferred: the utilisation of native rather than imported products and resources; an improvement in the balance of payments; the provision of new employment to absorb some portion of the natural increase and of the ever-replaced surplus of agricultural labour; national self-sufficiency. But the element of conscious policy in the several innovations was very small. Each undertaking was really occasioned by a particular crisis or demand. None sprang from a national plan or an articulated political philosophy. The constant factor which brought to birth one official creature after another was rather the basic ineffectiveness of domestic capitalism during the first decades of independence.

This casual beginning explains some characteristics of the state corporation in its early Irish form. Though the corporations had similarities to each other, no two constitutions or administrative arrangements were identical; and the relations between government and management were in no case clearly defined, but always turned to some extent upon the personalities concerned, and the degree of the corporation's success from time to time. There were, of course, very difficult problems in dual control: the extent to which the corporation should serve supposed national (sometimes a euphemism for party) interests; ministerial influence upon the managers' decisions; the use of profits or, less happily, the responsibility for deficits; security of tenure upon the supervisory board and for the main executives. In keeping with the Topsy-like growth of the new phenomenon, no serious analysis of the corporations' workings has been made; and generalisations about the resolution of these difficulties cannot be confidently framed. But this at least seems certain: that the problems were not answered by pre-devised formulae or pieces of constitutional machinery, but that they worked themselves out, if at all, according to the prevailing conditions in the organisation and politics. Perhaps the last British pragmatist will be found eventually on the south bank of the river Liffey!

But the British defence of pragmatism could be fairly made out in this instance. In general, the Irish state corporation operated with unexpected smoothness and efficiency. Some of this success must be attributed to its fitness for the social and economic environment in which it emerged. This is significant in at least two respects. Not only was Ireland long conditioned to a degree of state involvement in ordinary life well beyond her neighbour's, but these state enterprises were also able to provide opportunities for native managerial and entrepreneurial talent bereft of other outlets because of the smallness and the familial character of Irish commercial and industrial activity. Some of the most imaginative managers came from the army, civil service or local government organisations – the extraordinarily high calibre of many of the leading officers in all three being yet another epiphenomenon of the chronic under-employment in Ireland before 1960.

The state corporation has been discussed at such length not because it did or ever could transform the Irish economy by itself. It was not, even within its circumscribed range, immediately or universally successful; and it was never conceived of as an intrinsically superior economic form to the private business. It has been stressed because it was perhaps the most interesting and certainly the most original economic activity to emerge in the first generation after independence. Commonplace today, ventures like the Electricity Supply Board and the Sugar Company were *avant garde* when first established, all the more so because they owed nothing to revolutionary theory of any colour. They were also significant as illuminants of the peculiar social and economic needs of a former dependency, and as harbingers of the day when the state in Ireland would at last attempt a permanent rearrangement of the entire economy. Nearly forty years were to pass between the signing of the treaty and this radical departure; and in these forty years the official corporation was the first and perhaps the only significant whisper of the future.

The immediate precipitant of the economic *volte face*, the firm beginnings of which are to be placed in 1958–9, was a balance-of-payments crisis, with the concomitant credit restrictions, decline in employment and other symptoms of 'the British disease'. But the telling shock which both forced and enabled the government to embark upon a revolutionary programme was the level of emigration. In the mid-1950s the impression grew that a mass exodus of the Great Famine kind – not as great in absolute numbers of course, nor provoked by such terrible destitution, but of essentially the same variety – was at hand or had actually begun. To enter into this feeling, to understand the implications of emigration in the communal consciousness, we must recall in some detail and in the total historical context the experience of the preceding century – even if this involves a very long parenthesis.

In 1856 Sir James Stephen, reviewing the Irish emigration of the preceding decade and a half, observed that the mere figures, 'well weighed and meditated, will disclose a tragedy beyond the power of words to convey'. Without dwelling upon the tragedy, let us first meditate the broad patterns of Irish emigration before independence. During the nineteenth and earlier twentieth centuries nearly one Irishman in every three emigrated permanently. At any time between 1850 and 1900 more than 2 million Irish-born were living overseas, although the home population was dropping steadily. In round figures, 60 per cent of these millions would have been found in the

United States, 25 per cent in Great Britain, 5 per cent in British North America, 5 per cent in Australasia and the remaining 5 per cent in South Africa, other parts of the British Empire, South America and the Continent of Europe. In Ireland, all this meant a familial structure in which perhaps every second child migrated – from country to town, from town to city or, most commonly of all, beyond the seas. Children grew up in the fear or hope, the expectation or clear certainty, of leaving home or homeland. Inevitably, a certain air of impermanence pervaded Irish society: so much of it was provisional, preparatory.

Down to 1850 it may be fair to speak of the bulk of the Irish emigrants as uprooted. Generally, they were torn away, by irresistible economic forces, from a form of life to which they desperately clung. But in the second half of the century the term would be misleading. The roots holding the Irish to their soil had withered, except para- doxically in the poorest regions, the south-western and the western seaboards. For by the opening of the American Civil War, a very large number of Irish families were straddled across the Atlantic, with members on either side involved to some extent in common economic activity and social processes. The remittances of the members in North America furnished cash for rents and the means of paying for the passages of the latest to embark. Other social webs involved the same families with their members in Great Britain or flung in other places about the world. Beyond immediate blood relationship, the kin furnished more complex, if more thinly spun connections; and beyond the kin, the village or even larger localities occasionally provided some shadowy form of union. In structure at least, Irish society was ceasing to be Hiberno-centred.

In 1896 an Irish Race Convention was held in Dublin. Although partly a political device, the Convention did express the larger conception of nationality which had developed over the preceding half-century. Its promoters spoke of a 'race' of 20 million, only one quarter of which was left in Ireland. It is true that such a calculation assumed that the 'Irish' overseas were five times as numerous as the actual Irish-born abroad; it also ignored the existence of a very different conception of nationality among the Irish Unionists. But the imprecision and the extravagance do not mean that the new concept of race expressed no important reality. In fact, a high proportion of the Irish overseas – even of the second and third generations – thought of their allegiance as primarily to Ireland. Many others had mixed or multiple emotional commitments, with that to 'home' rising or falling according to the immediate political prospect. All this not only constituted a vast external reservoir of political power, but also formed, through invisible imports and easy access to alternative employment, a vital element in the post-famine Irish economy. The diaspora was a factor in some of the most important movements in industrialisation and urbanisation in the English-speaking countries, because of the quantity, the cheapness and the mobility of the labour which it contained. It set acute problems in assimilation or furnished a revivifying incursion of alien cells into fixed societies, according to one's point of view. As well as bitter grievances, it furnished deep social and psychological satisfactions to both sets of Irish.

To those at home the occasional eminence of the Irish overseas, as well as the more general manifestations of their capacity to thrive, soothed present humiliations and counteracted feelings of isolation and inferiority. To those abroad, often rejecting or rejected by their new environments, a people and a place to which they had ever 'belonged' was practically a necessity. Like the Jews, the Irish were extraordinary among non-coloured peoples for the persistence of their racial homogeneity; it is especially remarkable in that they had, in almost all cases, no language barrier to overcome. The explanation lay essentially in their religion and in their enmity. 'If an Irishman were brayed in a mortar', a nineteenth-century Irish bishop declared, 'two principles would be found indestructible – love of Catholicity and hatred of England, which last was tolerably synonymous with attachment to Ireland.' Of course, many Catholic emigrants abandoned their religion and more accepted the political and other orthodoxies of their new societies. But, speaking generally, the bishop's comment applied to the Irish outside as well as within the island.

It was not simply a matter of carrying preformed attitudes into exile. In each of the main regions of Irish immigration, anti-popery was a very powerful force in the nineteenth century. In the most important of these regions, the initial waves of Irish immigration threatened to undersell – often in fact undersold – native labour; this was another source of bitter recrimination, particularly in periods of depression. In all of these regions except one, allegiance to the British Crown was an established requirement; and even in the United States, anglophilia often reigned and a choice between the political interests of the new country and the old was occasionally forced upon the immigrants – even though few of the Irish-born were anxious to take out American citizenship. Everywhere, although in widely varied degrees according to time and place, Irish immigrants encountered positive hostility: their race, religion, poverty, historical experience and customary attitudes formed a compound more or less unpalatable to the majorities. A vicious (or virtuous, if one wishes) circle followed. Hostility increased the consciousness, and tended toward the perpetuation and even cherishing of separation. In-marriage and communal assertiveness deepened the hostility; time and the intrusion of much more exotic elements into the receiving societies gradually wore it down. But for the century 1840–1940, and more particularly for the sixty years 1860–1920, these antagonisms and identifications were prime factors in both the domestic and the inter-related histories of the English-speaking states.

It scarcely needs saying that they were important in the Anglo-Irish conflict. It is true that the influence of the Irish overseas – and in particular of the Irish-Americans – upon British policy in Ireland has been greatly exaggerated. There was one phase, 1916–17, with Great Britain abjectly dependent upon various American favours, when the Irish-Americans might have operated decisively. But at other junctures, and especially in the vital years 1919–21, there was really little prospect of their directly moving the United States government, let alone the British. On the other hand, they did help to shape 'world opinion', a vague and impalpable force perhaps, but also a significant one in the final crisis. British attitudes towards British conduct in Ireland – the crucial factor – were partly shaped by outside reactions. Moreover, without Irish-America, none of the fundamental late nineteenth-century movements, the parliamentary, the agrarian, or the Fenian, could have been developed upon a large scale; and, however wildly the sums were inflated by hysterical Tories, American dollars were at all stages a necessary underpinning for the Irish Party and the Republicans alike. The other areas of Irish settlement, especially Australasia, were also indispensable sources of finance, and even to some extent of moral pressure upon the imperial Parliament to reach an accommodation with the Irish. Thus the international Irish society, partly held together by an international church whose priesthood was constantly renewed from Ireland, was a major element in Irish nationalism and politics, no less than in Irish social and economic organisation, before the attainment of independence. It was also, of course, an important phenomenon in its own right.

After the treaty, 'overseas Ireland' declined rapidly in significance. Its political and economic bearing upon affairs in Ireland was reduced, and the entity itself disintegrated. In part, the decline was the natural and inevitable effect of time. (The question with the Irish communities overseas is not why they fell apart and were absorbed increasingly by their respective hosts, but why this process was delayed for two or even three generations beyond all normal expecta-tion.) In part, events in Ireland explain the change. First, although remittances and other 'invisible exports' arising from the Irish over-seas were by no means negligible in the Irish economy after 1920, the secular rise in living standards at home, and, more immediately, the Irish years of plenty during and immediately following the First World War, had greatly lessened their importance. The second, and really vital, factor was the Anglo-Irish settlement itself. It was their identification with a national struggle which had mobilised the Irish overseas: the extent of their assistance had always reflected the fortunes of the political contest at home, rising as success seemed closer, falling as the goal receded. With the achievement of independence, the Irish support movements lost their mainspring. For a few, the unwon Republic and the lost northern counties proved the need for continued action. But for the vast majority of the Irish overseas, the decisive conflict was over; substantially, the homeland had been freed. The agonies and confusion of the civil war added an element of disenchantment to the already general tendency toward disengagement.

All this robbed Irish emigration and the Irish communities overseas of political or romantic significance. No longer could emigration be presented as the evil fruit of British occupation, or invested with moving concepts of a folk-wandering, or with dreams of ultimate return. It sank to a mere issue of bread and butter. The mundane and dispiriting truth that the new state was incapable of maintaining her existing population, let alone absorbing her natural increase or calling back her exiles, seemed to have been established. Thus emigration changed, not its pace or its place in the Irish social pattern, but its character and meaning. It became the visible sign of failure – now of an interior failure in which the Irish people was wholly involved, and for which no outside scapegoat could be found.

In this matter of moods and attitudes, the crisis appears to have been reached in the middle 1950s. By then the net emigration was approaching 50,000 per annum, a level not far below the birth rate of the Republic; and considerably more than half of those reaching maturity were leaving the – apparently – stricken land. In the context of Irish emigration over the previous century and a half, these figures, though most disturbing, were not fantastic: at several junctures in the past they had been equalled or exceeded. But was this the context appropriate in the 1950s? It was now not a question of livelihoods for 7 or 6 or even 5 million within the twenty-six counties which constituted the Republic, but of maintaining a mere 3 million people or still less. Moreover, in each previous crisis of the same dimensions the absence of self-government could be blamed, and the departing could see themselves, and be seen by others, as the victims of colonialism. Again, the psychological aspects were perhaps more significant than ever before. Where there is no actual and immediate want, the contagion of impressions can be the determinant of emigration. In certain regions – the north-west midlands and north-east Connacht, for example – the sense of decay and premonitions of doom were overwhelming in the mid-1950s; it was all too easy to see here the first stages of a general depopulation, in which moreover, unlike the nineteenth-century exodus, there seemed no hope of subsequent resurrection.

To the present author, at any rate, emigration – still more, the current impression of emigration – was the very symbol of the malaise of 1956–8, which was of course also characterised by the familiar symptoms of balance of payments difficulties, credit restrictions, heavy unemployment and failing businesses. More than anything else, it was the sense of a growing flight from Ireland which prepared opinion for the heroic measures proposed by T. K. Whitaker, secretary to the department of finance, in a national plan published in 1958. Essentially, Whitaker's antidote was latter-day orthodoxy, a body of Keynesian solutions. But in a state remarkable for financial straitness of the older kind – the balanced budget, the instant response to short-term swings in the balance of payments, and the worship of thrift and caution – the plan implied a fair share of agonising reappraisal. Starting with the Republic's financial stability and strength, upon the one hand, and its miserable rate of growth, upon the other, Whitaker proposed to exploit the first in order to advance the second. This ultimately implied that the government should drive the commercial banks, which still influenced economic policy profoundly by striving to maintain their own external strength, towards supporting national expansion as the over-riding economic object. At the same time, the Central (or state) Bank's powers of financial direction, hitherto very small, would have to be enlarged. Next, the government's own expenditure should be channelled, so far as possible, into directly productive rather than socially useful undertakings. Here the public corporation and the earlier state involvement in capitalistic enterprise had long before prepared the way for bolder and more deliberate participation. But private investment was distinguished as the most critical area of all; and this was to be encouraged and guided by a development programme, laying down priorities in, and orderly sequences of, investment, and concentrating in particular on the nurturing of the export industries.

It must not be supposed that 'Whitakerism' flashed quite unheralded on to the scene. As has been said above, not only did the state corporation already furnish one of the necessary instruments of direction, but it also tacitly recognised government's creative function in organising the national resources. Other partial anticipations studded the earlier decades. The report of the Fiscal Inquiry Committee of 1923, certain of Fine Gael's agricultural policies in the

1920s, the Control of Manufactures Act of 1932 and the establishment of the Industrial Development Authority twenty years later all foreshadowed one facet or other of the 1958 proposals. But even the sum of these numerous part-precedents and premonitory signs does not destroy the revolutionary character of Whitaker's plan. For the plan was, to a degree hitherto unknown in Ireland, comprehensive, rational and coherent. It embraced the whole economy; it argued from set economic principles and scales of economic value; and each of its parts was consistent with its companions and subordinated to an over-riding aim. This is not meant to suggest that the plan soared high above all criticism from economists – what plan could? – or that it regarded every corner of the Irish economy with equal coolness. But it was a systematic and sustained attempt to subject the entire problem to modern analysis, and as such it was unprecedented. It is important to avoid too heroic and too catastrophic a view of the result. But to treat it merely as the final stage in a steady chain of development would be still more misleading.

The Whitaker plan proved to be the prelude to the first economic programme, adopted in 1959, the year in which de Valera retired at last from active politics, which he had bestridden like a Colossus for more than four decades. There was, of course, an ultimate connection between the two events. Although Lemass, the new prime minister, was also a veteran of the Easter Rising, his interests had long lain in the material rather than the abstract elements of Irish nationality, and in the prospective rather than the past. He spoke the same language as the young men born or grown to manhood after 1923, of whom Whitaker himself was an example. Although it is a dangerous concept to handle, certain stages are best categorised as the supersession of one generation by another: 1880 may very plausibly be represented as such a watershed in Irish history; 1916 as a second. Perhaps we are too close to the event to make a judgement, but all the evidence to hand suggests that 1959 also marked a decisive change in national power and attitude. If politically 1959 seemed to stand for a species of ecumenicism to which the separated brethren of the north-east gradually responded (and to which, despite all, in certain senses and circles they continue to respond), economically it stood for a change of heart and will. 'In our present circumstances', said the first economic programme, 'we must be prepared to take risks under all headings – social, commercial and financial – if we are to succeed in the drive for expansion.' It proceeded to put into force Whitaker's original recommendations, to establish a series of new public bodies specifically concerned with development, and to attempt to attract foreign capital and manufacturing techniques to the Republic by a system of 'tax holidays' and other forms of indirect subsidisation, especially favourable for the export industries. The goal specified in the 1959 programme was modest: the growth rate was to be doubled; but since this implied a rise from 1 to 2 per cent, the authors could scarcely be charged with wild ambition.

The success of the first programme astonished friend and foe alike. The growth rate of 1959–64, the period of the first programme, was 4 instead of 2 per cent. In the same years, the GNP rose by nearly 25 per cent and exports by more than 40 per cent. Investment was almost doubled, despite the fact that savings also increased. The social revolution was no less dramatic. The population of the Republic had fallen, in an almost unbroken line from 6·5 million in 1841 to 2·8 million in 1961. But in 1961–6 it actually increased by 2·3 per cent, while the net emigration dropped to 16,000, about one-third of the level of the preceding decade. Still more significant was the change in the structure of the population revealed by the census of 1966. The largest increase was in the 20–24 age group, which had grown by nearly 25 per cent. The 10–14 and 15–19 groups also showed remarkable increases. In effect, this meant, if current trends continued, that the proportion of those reaching maturity who would be absorbed in the Republic was 75 per cent, not far short of double the proportion who remained at home in the years 1950–9. Moreover, the marriage rate was bound to change dramatically. The extra-ordinarily low rate of 5·5 per thousand, a long-established factor in Irish society, would probably increase by 2·0 per thousand in the coming decade. The renewal of life and hope might be discerned even in the face of the country. Not merely in the urban areas as a whole, but also in no less than a quarter of the countryside, the population increased by over 7 per cent in 1961–6. In the remaining rural areas, the decline was reduced to 4 per cent, a no less remarkable achieve-ment. The fundamental explanation was industrial growth, planned development radiating outward from the selected centres, mineral discovery and the systematic reorganisation of agriculture and tourism. In few other Western nations would these statistics seem especially encouraging even in crude terms of economic growth, but in the Republic they proclaimed a 'miracle'. Correspondingly, there cannot be many Western countries where, in recent years, the advent of factory industry, or the rapid augmentation of the money supply, or the reversal of a secular decline in population, would be taken as particularly cheering developments. But neither had many such countries a matching experience of contraction and decay, generation by generation, or an equal degree of misery amongst the very poor.

While the first programme still ran its course, foundations for the second, to cover the years 1964–70, were being laid. New planning bodies, concerned with industrial organisation and development in its social as well as its economic context, reported on the current practice and performance of Irish business, on manpower, and on future planning. In each case, further public authorities were established: 'adaptation councils' to modernise particular industries; a Manpower Authority to deploy labour resources, re-train and re-settle workers, and increase individual productivity; and committees to plan second-stage development, and to co-ordinate as exactly as possible the functions of government, capital, and labour in the various areas of the projected industrial advance. The second economic programme accepted the now familiar growth rate of over 4 per cent as a basis, and aimed at further heroic increases in the export trades. In Ireland exports truly were the alpha and the omega of growth, because of the minuteness of the domestic market – less than 3 million persons in the Republic. Even if Northern Ireland were included (for the sake of geographical propriety, if nothing else) well under 5 million would be involved.

Having already committed itself to the 'Kennedy Rounds' of general tariff reductions, the Republic next entered into a special free trade agreement with Great Britain at the end of 1965. By this, Great Britain undertook to abolish, almost immediately, all charges on all imports from the Republic, and to increase substantially the Irish share of the British market for butter, bacon, livestock and other agricultural products. In return, the Republic agreed to dismantle all tariff barriers against British goods, and to withdraw the tax incentives and other subsidies for foreign industrialists, stage by stage, over fifteen years. Thus the wheel was to come full circle by 1980. Sixty years after the treaty, the British Isles would once again become a free trade area; economically, the Act of Union would be restored! But of course the assumption was that the conditions of the nineteenth and early twentieth centuries would meanwhile have disappeared, that the Irish national economy would soon be strong enough, in the sectors in which it was sensible to concentrate its efforts and resources, to compete effectively in the world at large. Various secondary industries, especially of the assemblage variety, which have been built up under the shelter of protection to promote employment and 'self-sufficiency', would doubtless go to the wall. But this did not mean – according to the planners – that the status quo ante bellum would return. Political independence was to be used positively in the coming fifteen years to revolutionise the Irish social, agrarian and industrial structures, and so to develop the inherent human, locational and climatic assets, that the Republic could live and thrive in open international competition.

> He either fears his fate too much,
> Or his deserts are small,
> That dares not put it to the touch
> To win or lose it all.

The latest venture on the board has been, of course, the decision to enter the European Economic Community. This is the ultimate speculation. Niagara has now been shot.

And will they, economically speaking, live happily ever after? There is no ever-afterwards; and not only the ultimate fate but even the immediate significance of the economic revolution initiated in 1959 are matters which a twenty-first and not a twentieth-century historian should determine. Even as things stand now, the devil's advocate does not lack material for his brief. He might argue that the expansion in the Irish economy since 1959 has occurred in a period of world boom, and that because of her extraordinary dependence upon exports, Ireland is particularly sensitive to world economic movements, and particularly vulnerable in a protracted international downturn. He might point to the fact that despite the new prosperity Irish unemployment, 6 per cent at lowest and reaching up to 10, has remained very high by Western European standards, and add that because of the complete mobility of labour within the British Isles, Irish wage levels always correspond to British, regardless of the respective productivity in the two islands or of the effects on Irish costs per unit. Moreover – and let us abandon our depressing advocate and write directly – the first economic programme enjoined the Irish people to take risks, and risks imply the possibility of failure. Even what has been achieved has not been painless. Inevitably, certain groups in Irish society have slipped on the social and economic ladder; inevitably, certain ventures have proved rash. The Irish economy and the fiscal system are still enmeshed with Britain's, and if Great Britain proves to be the chronic Sick Man of the Western world, the Republic cannot hope to avoid the illness. A basic presupposition of the leap forward of the 1960s was that sooner or later Ireland, in both its parts, would be absorbed in the Common Market. And who can yet predict the economic consequences of this boldness? The ultimate object and the indispensable prerequisite of the programmes was the generation of confidence. But confidence is fragile: if it can create its own momentum in prosperity, there is the opposite dynamism in adversity – as the events of the middle 1950s sadly showed.

Finally, does not Irish history, seen in certain lights, seem to be one of dreams destroyed?

I sought a hall.
And, behold! – a change
From light to darkness, from joy to woe!
King, nobles, all,
Looked aghast and strange;
The minstrel-group sate in dumbest show!
Had some great crime
Wrought this dread amaze,
This terror? None seemed to understand . . .
I again walked forth;
But lo! the sky
Showed fleckt with blood, and an alien sun
Glared from the north,
And there stood on high,
Amid his shorn beams, a skeleton!

Mangan's lines were written not much short of a century and a half ago.

But as we compose this doleful catalogue we should also remember that there is no economy under the sun without elements making for gloom, and none, in the nature of the case, which can hope for – if indeed it should be hoped for instead of feared – permanent stability; and when we talk of the 'risks' of 1959, we should consider too the dispiriting alternative. To have maintained the courses set since 1945 would have been, so far as it is possible to see, ruinous. Perhaps there is, as Walpole said, a deal of ruin in a nation. But the Republic in the later 1950s was surely exhausting its supplies. Moreover, what was achieved in 1959–72 was not merely the attainment of the first goal in a long economic race. It was also in itself a completed feat. For the first time in more than a century, the most powerful, that is, the retrogressive, trends in Irish social and economic life had been reversed. For the first time since 1921, Irish governments had tried wholeheartedly to use their freedom to win freedom in the economic as well as the political and ideological senses. After all, what was being capitalised under the programmes was the independent power to pursue, so far as might be, the national economic good. This power was inherent in the treaty, but ill-used and borne down by other aims and by 'the gale of the world' in earlier years. Never before 1959 was the total mobilisation and redeployment of the national resources seriously attempted. But what has been done since that date cannot be undone. Perhaps this is to say that hope is now a permanent possession. May it be so, at least.

7

Old Lamps for New

I

The author lived out of Ireland for the twenty years 1948–68, and wrote the original book in Australia in 1966–7. It might be supposed that it was some lemming-like instinct which induced him, as a historian, to return to his subject on the eve of its reactivation. If so, it was a humbling experience. Even the mild hopes expressed in 1967 that there was now a 'living generation' in Ireland, or that hope itself was at last a permanent possession, soon seemed so many mockeries; each year, and at times each month, brought new and deeper reasons for despair. In black hours, it appeared that there was nothing left for any rational inhabitant of the island but to write Yeatsian poetry *à la* 1919–21, if only he had the talent. Moreover, it was the day of the instantaneous. The course of events so twisted and darted, at times, that yesterday seemed irrelevant by mid-day and tomorrow unknowable at nightfall. The babble of explanation was too loud for thought, and, in immediate exposition and analysis, the best of the journalists proved themselves superior to the scholars. But after all it is one's business to ply one's trade. I do not mean by this that the historian should try now to write the history of 1968–73, still less that he should indicate the future. As one of the characters in *Let Dons Delight* observed, 'Prophecy is a mug's game'. At any rate, it is not a historian's. Still, whether or not Macaulay's New Zealander would, later on, have sketched the ruins of London, Macaulay himself would certainly have scribbled in the midst of the catastrophe he envisaged. He might not – certainly, he should not – have attempted to write its history. But he could not have helped expressing himself historically about it.

To have continued all the themes in the original volume over the half-a-dozen years since 1967 would have meant another book, and called for a seer to write it. Ireland, in both its parts (to take one instance) entered the Common Market towards the close of that short period. But the leap in the dark seemed, immediately, no more than a jump from the bottom doorstep; and there was very little initial encouragement for the belief or fear that national identities might be gradually subsumed into 'higher' allegiances. But decades, or generations, are the contexts here; their passage must simply be awaited. Again, there have been signs that the inherited structure of permanent government in the Republic is being modified. When county managers traverse their domains opening bridges and libraries like bishops, and assistant secretaries publicly defend departmental policy at open meetings in provincial towns, and local government officers are public partisans in conservation-and-industry disputes, the historic distinction between the political and the bureaucratic seems blurred, to say the least. But what have we here: aberration or the supersession of one form of polity by another? It is much too soon to say whether the phenomenon is explicable in terms of a new generation of public servants, not reared in the values of the British Treasury, or as another crop of the 'overmighty subjects' of which there are so many examples from Chadwick to Morant in British administrative history itself, or as an adjustment to new forms of social management made necessary by developments in knowledge or techniques of mass control or mass participation. In politics proper, there are similar puzzling innovations. What did Mr de Valera, for example, think of a successor Taoiseach who defended himself against charges of wasting public money on an air journey, made partly at least for state purposes, by pointing out that his fare had been paid by an oil company? What of an Irish public opinion which received such an explanation not merely complacently, but with (to all appearances) positive satisfaction? On the other hand, what state enduring parliamentary government in 1968–73 could not produce cases as bizarre, according to the *mores* of yesterday? Whether or not they are the heralds of fundamental change, it is as yet impossible to say.

Any of these or perhaps other fields may conceivably seem to the twenty-first-century historian of the late 1960s and early 1970s more significant than 'the northern question'. But to people of today that question seems so massive and ramifying that it must dominate any brief consideration of the recent past in Ireland. In this chapter an attempt will be made, not to write the history of the latest years in any sense whatever, but to speculate historically about their northern aspect. The most fruitful questions to raise seem to the present writer to be: what past patterns of Irish political behaviour, what past patterns of Irish political ideology and what past patterns of

British policy towards Ireland throw most light upon the present, and are in turn illuminated by it? To these three questions the remainder of this chapter *seriatim* is addressed.

II

The tradition of alternative government in Ireland, although foreshadowed earlier, dates effectively from the Whiteboy movement of the early 1760s.[1] This was the first concerted and powerful counter to the increasing burden of tithes, raised rents, enclosures and spreading pasturage which marked the mid-eighteenth century. Peasant counter-action was of course a common phenomenon in Western Europe at this time. But in few other places – perhaps in none – did it exhibit the regularity, persistence and comprehensiveness of Ireland: there it rose well above the level of cyclical and circling food riots. In Ireland (to use the English contrast, for example) labourers bore tithes, had no poor law to fall back on and could hope for little from town or industrial employment. Under pressure, their state was proportionately the more desperate.

Whiteboyism was distinguished from similar movements abroad and earlier movements in Ireland by three features. It was oath-bound and conspiratorial in form; it relied upon mass support or at least mass neutrality, and sought to use the pressure of numbers to secure its ends; and it aimed at stabilising and rendering permanent various economic and other relationships within society. The first of these features led on naturally to harsh internal and external discipline, and quasi-military forms. Whiteboy punishments of wayward members, resisters and transgressors of their code were usually swift and cruel. Doubtless, they were also occasionally a cover for personal vengeance or extortion. In short, they represented the private counterpart of the public 'justice' of an eighteenth-century state. We know comparatively little of the command structure or internal organisation of the Whiteboy movement, but this much at least is clear: that it involved a captaincy system, the building up of arms and on occasions quite sophisticated tactical planning – not to mention uniforms and intimidatory display in favourable circumstances.

But Whiteboy violence and intimidation were directed quite as much towards the enlistment or implication of large numbers in the movement as to direct and immediate objects. 'Swearing-in' of other peasants took place (under threat or persuasion) on isolated farms at night or on estates before the general expiration of leases or, most commonly of all perhaps, after Sunday mass, when all in the parish were collected and particularly vulnerable to demands to constitute a common front. In 1786 in fact the Bishop of Ossory attempted to check the spread of conspiracy by closing all chapels and suspending mass in his diocese for a time. All this had of course two purposes: first, to ensure the Maoist sea for the fish to swim in, and secondly (and most important strategically) to frighten authority into concession by the terrifying prospect of numberless masses ranged behind the demands.

Finally, although the movement grew out of particular instances of tithe increases and enclosures of common land in County Tipperary, it soon developed, as it swept backwards and forwards in later years across Munster and South Leinster, a very wide range of objects. In sum, they fell little short of a political programme. The regulation of rents, leases and tithes were the most common aims, but employment and wages, food and other prices, county cess, tolls, hearth money and birth, marriage and death dues to the Catholic clergy were also areas of struggle. Whiteboyism then, by that or any other name, constituted an effort, not to win political power or religious parity, but to deploy countervailing force for economic ends. These ends were conservative. Rents, tithes, dues, tolls, taxes and the rest were not assailed in themselves, but accepted as elements in a received social order. It was innovation, arbitrariness and above all what seemed to be exorbitance which were resisted. It was (in E. P. Thompson's phrase) the 'moral economy' of the masses, their concept of the right relations between landlord and tenant, farmer and labourer, producer and consumer, purveyor and customer, which they sought to maintain or re-establish. The *locus classicus* of successful Whiteboyism was the campaign of 1786 to force Catholic bishops and priests to reduce ecclesiastical charges to amounts set unilaterally by the movement. Not only did the bishops yield on this: like so many latter-day vice-chancellors, they arranged the removal of the most obnoxious of their subordinates and promised 'to investigate all causes of complaint'.

As the 1786 campaign suggests, the Whiteboys were originally free from sectarianism. In fact, in the earliest years, Protestants were quite often to be found as members and even captains. But as the movement crept northwards to Meath, Louth and the present Ulster border counties in the 1780s, its character changed. It was readily adaptable to defending the particular economic interests of either the Protestant or the Catholic community, where they saw themselves ranged against each other, and more or less on a level socially and close in numbers. In one sense it was the Protestant small farming class which resembled more closely the original movement. Although it was the Catholics who appropriated the title Defenders – and the

Defenders did indeed act at times as a bulwark against physical and psychological assault – it was the Protestant Oakboys who really represented the preservative idea inherent in early Whiteboyism. As Catholics competed ever more effectively for leases and employment, Protestants saw the traditional order threatened by aggrandisement from below. For Whiteboyism proper the aggrandisement had come from above; but, this apart, the northern Protestant conspiracy was a repetition of the Munster one. It too sought the re-establishment of a 'moral economy' and by much the same organisation, methods and forms of force. Much the same was true of orangeism in the succeeding decade. In many regards, the Orangemen were the natural successors of the Protestant Whiteboys. Both were concerned with social and economic dislocation – albeit from a single, simple source. It was the same sudden exorbitance and the same vision, or rather nightmare, of role reversal which brought both into and kept both in being. *Plus ça change. . . .*

It would be wrong to regard all these movements as mere 'protests'. On the contrary, it was their special mark to be regulatory. Many late eighteenth- and early nineteenth-century observers noted that Ireland was a peculiarly 'lawless' country, not merely in terms of crimes of violence, but also in the extent to which the legal system of the state was distrusted and abhorred. But the most acute, Arthur Young, de Tocqueville and Nassau Senior, went on to emphasise the element of alternative government – of a rival legal code and rival law enforcement – implicit in Whiteboyism and its successors. A further refinement of the same matter is that the allegiance of even the beneficiaries of a partial and partisan administration of Dublin Castle was contingent, not absolute. Throughout the nineteenth century signs were abundant that Irish Protestants felt the chill of alienation from the state, and were prepared to travel some distance along the road of rejection of the state, when government or law appeared to favour their sectarian antagonists. Home Rule itself had such an origin; and after 1830 there were various occasions on which Protestant Ulster's determination not to be governed through the public opinion of Great Britain was foreshadowed. Not for nothing did a leading Belfast newspaper keep emblazoned at its head, *Pro rege saepe, pro patria semper.*

Thus, on every hand Ireland was subject or at least susceptible to the notion of an extra-legal government or law which must, in extremities, supersede and even oust the formal and official order. Just as the Irish question was basically a colonial question, so Irish society was basically a frontier society. In each case, geographical contiguity to Great Britain, the imposed constitutional structure of a unitary state, and the theory of equal citizenship, rendered it a peculiarly complex form of colonial question and frontier society. Still, frontier law was ever and everywhere on the prowl. It is better to say 'law' than 'lawlessness', for it was a multi-legal society rather than a lawless one. The codes developed by the recalcitrant communities had, from their very Whiteboy beginnings in 1761, formal procedures, rules of equity, known scales of penalties and even ceremonies – however grotesque. Of course, under pressure, the corruption which violence breeds and the evil men it beckons, these codes repeatedly degenerated. But the *idea* of such a system, expressing and enforcing a superior justice and a swifter retribution than the Crown's justices and policemen would ever furnish, kept rising out of the ruins of particular failures.

Over predominantly Catholic Ireland (roughly coterminous with the present Republic) the relationship of Whiteboyism and its descendants and both the constitutional and revolutionary political movements of 1801–1922 was both intricate and ambivalent. Sooner or later every constitutional party, from O'Connell's to Redmond's, condemned and dissociated itself from peasant law, as a force which was imperilling the national objectives. There were corresponding condemnations, for corresponding reasons, from every radical-revolutionary organisation, from the Young Ireland left to the refurbished IRB. Sooner or later, all repudiated Whiteboyism as both disgraceful and diversionary. Yet, to a degree, both the constitutional and the violent parties were the heirs, and even the derivatives of the Whiteboys. It was the renewal and intensification of Whiteboyism in the early 1820s which made loud the unuttered threat of mass disorder to which Peel and Wellington surrendered in 1828–9. It was a further outburst which broke the established tithe system in the next decade. It was the Land League that gave Parnell the bricks for building. It was 'the last hurrah' of Whiteboyism in the west, in 1898–1900, which provided the driving force of the United Irish League, and might well have carried the reconstituted Irish Party into a new radicalism. Moreover, the strategy of all O'Connell's campaigns – the model for subsequent 'constitutional' agitation – was to intimidate by producing a vast (if possible the illusion of a universal) combination in support of specific legislative objects. Armed force apart, what was this but an expression, in daylight and upon a national scale, of what Whiteboys had striven to effect, darkly and in localities, for half a century? Similarly, it scarcely needs saying that both the United Irishmen of 1798 and the Fenian movement were sitting enthroned upon Whiteboyism in the countryside. It was critical in the growth of each to find a population habituated to conspiracy, swearing in, arms seizures and the rest. It was, to use a wry comparison, the counterpart of the priests taking over from the landlords, in 1826–8, the direction of the forty-shilling freeholders reared to vote *en bloc*. After all, the substitution was neither difficult nor unnatural. The republicans, in every generation, were aiming at a 'moral polity', which mirrored the peasants' 'moral economy' at every point except objective. Sinn Fein was the supreme expression of the 'moral polity'; the military methods of its instrument after 1917, the IRA, were *mutatis mutandis* those of 1761.

Of course, with the 1916 Rising we enter a phase in which both the idea and the apparatus of alternative government have become more extensive, sophisticated and powerful. The crisis here came when the Provisional Government of 1922 took over the formal state structure from Great Britain to the accompaniment of a fresh alternative government and another 'moral polity' to challenge the real. De Valera's entry into the Dail in 1927 and the peaceful transference of power to Fianna Fail in 1932 were decisive stages in the decline of the new anti-state and anti-law in the south. But so long as the moral reality of a republic, with true, though prudentially suspended, jurisdiction over the entire island, was officially asserted, it was impossible to root out entirely the notion of alternative government. If the authority of the Dail over its twenty-six counties were actively and directly challenged by the IRA or otherwise, the challenge had sooner or later to be met. But if the challenge were to Stormont only, things were much more awkward. Received doctrine, natural sympathy and the inherited patterns of behaviour and scale of evaluation all meant that, in a certain degree and specific area, a refined and politicised Whiteboyism still survived.

Ironically, the final exorcism – or so at least it seemed at the time to the present author – came during 1970–2. The various efforts of those years, from the attempted gun-running of 1970 to the Bloody Sunday demonstrations and burning of the British Embassy in 1972, to draw both state and society in the Republic into a more clearly avowed and active support for 'alternative government' in Northern Ireland seemed to be placing parliamentary order in grave peril. Retrospectively, some might say, with Condé in the French wars of religion, 'We should have been destroyed, had we not been so near destruction'. As the implications of interventionism for their own social harmony and economic order became apparent, the great body of citizens in the Republic recoiled from such a course. Even if they would not endorse the old state or current statelessness in Northern Ireland, they decidedly repudiated the 'anti-state' there in all its manifestations. Forced to choose, they surrendered the vestigial remains of the Whiteboy spirit. It had become too dangerous an emotional indulgence. At any rate, this seemed to be the very clear implication of the referenda and general election, and many other happenings in the Republic, in 1972–3.

In Northern Ireland, however, the effect of the Government of Ireland Act of 1920 was to stiffen and virtually institutionalise Whiteboy stances. It is notorious that the Catholic community (the professional classes to a limited extent excluded) was and remained 'disloyal'. Not merely in such fields as education and hospitals, but even in sport, drinking, commerce and most other forms of social coalescence, they persisted in counter-systems. Their 'state', if any, lay outside their borders; and when the Dublin regime proved to be the god that failed, they attempted to create, so far as might be, self-governing and mass-governed enclaves – the *ultima thule* of any Whiteboy movement. But all this was scarcely less true of Protestants, again with the partial exception of the university educated. So long as formal government and law enforcement coincided more or less with the Protestant 'moral polity', they identified themselves with these substantially. But when the formal government seemed to furnish inadequate protection for the accustomed social hierarchy and distributions, they took to the streets to check the 'exorbitance'. Annually, they took pains to demonstrate their mass power and communal will to maintain the established demarcations and ascendancies.

It would hardly be disputed – though almost everything else may be – that the very serious threat to this entire moral order, which the reforming spirit of the 1960s represented, was a major precipitant of Ulster's current conflicts. In ironic inversion of the dictum that revolutions spring from rising living standards and political liberalisation, a counter-revolution sprang from the same developments where the dominant sections constituted a democratic majority. Perhaps it was dreaded prospects rather than actual encroachments to that date which generated this reaction. No matter: the 'moral economy' and 'moral polity' alike seemed to be on the point of crumbling under the formal state. Hence, it appeared imperative either to force the state back into support of the traditional order, or else to look to alternative government and law.

When, after further turns in the cycle of thrust and counter-thrust, Stormont was suspended, each population in Northern Ireland found itself in a new and perplexing situation. For unionists, it was a question whether some new regional assembly, an independent state (or dominion) or 'integration' with Great Britain promised now to save most – or lose least – of the old order. For nationalists, the question was precisely the same, but upside down, with 'integration' with the Republic as their third alternative. For both communities, the concept of 'alternative government' was adrift. Such a concept is of its nature antithetical, and meaningful only in the context of a formally established and palpable state. What was the 'state' in Northern Ireland after March 1972? All was provisional. Unless the evidence of the day were altogether misleading, it was impossible to suppose that Great Britain any longer desired to maintain an Irish presence, let alone manage (as she was now forced to attempt) an Irish government. Moreover, 'alternative government' had taken on new meanings. The accompanying violence had rendered it a Frankenstein's monster. Violence had taken on a life of its own, independent of its original purpose. Safeguarding the machinery of 'safeguarding' the community was rapidly becoming an end in itself. In short, to the mass of Protestants and Catholics alike, Whiteboyism was failing, as all else had failed. Yet the matrix of the Whiteboy spirit, the contrast between the 'moral polities' and the actual, remained, and remains. There is multiple alienation without, any longer, a sharply defined alienator. Even intra-communal consensus appears to have disintegrated under the strains, quite markedly in the Protestant community, but to a degree in both. *Destruo et aedificabo* perhaps – it seems all that there is to hope for, at any rate.

III

What has been crammed together under the title 'Whiteboy' is an indigenous element in Irish history which has proved remarkably enduring and resilient over the past two centuries. Few societies have failed to produce a rough equivalent to Whiteboyism at some stage or stages in their development. But it is none the less true that this particular form of the spirit and impulse, and its practical manifestations, were peculiar to Ireland, and persist and recur extraordinarily there. In political ideology, on the other hand, modern Ireland was for a century, broadly speaking, a borrower – however laggard and wayward – from continental Europe. To a degree which would surprise those who have not thought much about the matter, it reflected the changes in mood and emphasis in the Western world at large from the late eighteenth to the late nineteenth century.

The first great shaping influence of recent times was the enlightenment, which struck Ireland late but heavily in the 1780s and 1790s. It may be, as Professor May has argued, that the principles common to the enlightenment everywhere and in all forms were few and highly generalised: that the current age was more rational, humane and undeceived than any in the past, or that truth comes to us from without through our natural faculties, and not from interior illumination. None the less, the enlightenment did produce a distinctive and unmistakable cast of mind, and was strongly marked by rationalism, atomism and universalism in its approach to politics. Grattan was perhaps the first considerable enlightenment man in Irish politics. But he expressed its moderate, balancing, temporising English version. An oligarch and anglophile, he was already out of tune with the democratic and self-determining surge in Irish radicalism in the 1790s. His 'people' were to be few in number and substantial in status; he differentiated them sharply from the rabble. He did not hesitate for a moment in committing Ireland to Britain's war in 1793, and never withdrew a support which he took to be automatic. Such whiggery, for all its gallant striving after personal freedoms, parliamentary honesty, free trade or 'national' self-respect, was practically irrelevant to the Ireland of the future.

Far otherwise in the case of the two other very considerable men of the enlightenment in Irish politics, Tone and O'Connell. In conventional Irish historiography, Tone and O'Connell are made to stand in opposition as rival fountain-heads of rival traditions of resistance. The one is taken to symbolise physical revolution and abstract republicanism (with socialism, somewhat improbably, added lately), the other, moral force, parliamentarianism, empiricism and negotiation. What is quite forgotten (it seems to the present author) is that both Tone's and O'Connell's traditions derived from the same master ideology of the enlightenment. They represented different emphases, the one millenarian and eschatalogical, the other, pragmatic and gradual, within a single general European movement. They shared critically important assumptions about the nature of political behaviour. Both took it for granted that society is an artefact rather than an organism. Both took it for granted that politics concern the conscious and the rational. Both assumed that liberty consists in an absence, the absence of suppressions and restraints: any process of liberation was for them, therefore, negative, the removal of clogs and distorting pressures. Above all, it would have seemed self-evident to both that colour, creed and similar apparently divisive social elements are but superficial distinctions, which liberty, education and freed reason would quickly dissipate. From Tone and O'Connell alike, then, two vital Irish nationalist assumptions derive – first, that the end of domination will produce an automatic resolution of domestic political tensions; the other, that Irish nationality is synonymous with Irish residence, and that once Ireland is released from domination, common residence will dwarf and render quite insignificant all other confessional, occupational or economic variations.

From the circumstances of Tone's career came the notion of an insurrectionary or catastrophic climax to the struggle for independence. From the circumstances of O'Connell's career came a peculiar form of parliamentarianism and popular participation. O'Connell's parliamentarianism was willy-nilly a politics of resistance. The struggle for parity within an obdurately hostile political environment tended to produce, on the one hand, a sort of boss system, based on favour, jobbery and reward, and on the other hand, constitutional obstruction and negation. But these very different and important ulterior emphases should not be allowed to obscure the fact that Tone's and O'Connell's starting points were identical, or that they were products of a common culture and shared a set of fundamental values.

It is as true as it is ironical that it proved impossible for O'Connell to conduct campaign after campaign for religious parity in Ireland without producing a religious confrontation and something of a politico-religious polarisation. It is true that his instinctive sympathies and antipathies occasionally, and increasingly, surged over his principles; and that, at the end, the political necessity of harnessing the episcopate to his movements forced him on to several sectarian courses. Correspondingly, it is true that, early and late, Tone was a political corsair, and that he finally appealed (in the little phrase in which so much has been erected in recent years) to 'the men of no property'. But if we consider their great careers as totalities, the deviations from the corpus of enlightened principles appear few and trivial. Almost always, they were forced upon them by gnarled realities. It was not by choice that Tone called upon the propertyless to act or O'Connell accepted kingship of the beggars. They did so only after the 'classes' had failed them.

The second master influence on the formation of the Irish nationalist mind was German Romanticism. Here the most critical single event seems to have been Thomas Davis's visit to Germany in 1839–40.[2] Davis underwent an evangelical-like conversion when confronted by the works of Lessing, Fichte and the Schlegels and by the example of Prussia whose genius, he wrote, having 'tossed in a hot trance, sprung up fresh and triumphant', as soon as she had halted the advance of the French – culturally as well as militarily. Under these visions, Davis's conventional radicalism slipped away, to be replaced by the German Romantics' assumption that national culture, national history and national language were not merely ornamental, but integral, to national identity. But two deviations from the strict German model were forced on Davis by his circumstances. First, the culture to be rejected and resisted was, in Ireland's case, not French but English: hence Davis's denunciations of Utilitarianism, Industrialism and Urbanisation, much in the same strain as *Rural Rides*, the Tractarians, the Romantic Tories or *Hard*

Times. Where O'Connell opposed the retention of the Irish language as a barrier to economic development, modernisation and education, Davis was anxious to revive it precisely because it was a barrier – to anglicisation. Secondly, Davis could not follow the German model in stressing either religion or racial purity in the genetic sense: all else apart, this would have left him stranded. Hence, for example, his observation on the Wexford men of 1798 that 'though their blood was for the most part English and Welsh . . . yet they were Irish through and through in thought and feeling'. At the same time, these two deviations help us to understand how Davis could be, and can be, placed, however misleadingly, in a line of ideological succession from Tone downwards. There were apparent similarities in the two cries to break the connection with England and in the two declarations that Catholic, Protestant and Dissenter formed a single flock. But Tone's and Davis's words had very different provenances and contexts. The apparent or verbal similarities should not blind us to the revolution which Romanticism had really wrought. The new emphasis was on *cultural* division and *cultural* hostility; on emotion rather than rationality; on group rights rather than individual; on a subjective and creative rather than a formal and negative concept of independence; and, of course, in the very long run, on race and language, as in the Fatherland. In essentials, Young Ireland was the harbinger of Ireland after Parnell, of the New Ireland of the 1890s.

In one significant respect, Young Ireland remained ambivalent, where German Romanticism had moved decisively in the 1840s. This was the attitude to be adopted towards 'modernisation'. Generally, the German left embraced it, just as they came generally to embrace a *Kleindeutsch* solution to the problem of unification. Davis and the *Nation* often envisaged Ireland as a modern nation state and, like Sir Robert Kane, counted her undeveloped industrial, mineral and maritime resources. But all this was indefinite and amateurish, without any understanding or perhaps knowledge of modern science, technology or manufacturing processes or organisation. It was besides more than counteracted by the persistent vision of a nation of small-holders, and an idealisation of the peasant. Not for nothing did the *Nation* proclaim itself 'racy of the soil'. Moreover, the tendency to identify the abhorred anglicisation with urbanisation, commercialism and mechanisation was already very strong. An excellent expression of the attitude occurs, fifty years on, in a passage of dialogue in Sheehan's *Luke Delmege*:

'I never think of England but as in that dream of Piranesi – vast Gothic halls, machinery, pulleys, and all moving with the mighty, rolling mechanism that is crushing into a dead monotony all the beauty and picturesqueness of the world.'

'That is, bringing it up to a level of civilisation and culture,' said Luke.

'And why did the Almighty create the Afghan and the Ashantee, to be turned, in the course of time, into a breeched and bloated Briton? . . . England's mission is to destroy and corrupt everything she touches – '

The roots of the rejection of modernisation and the simultaneous search for and cultivation of the primitive and elemental in Irish life are to be found in the Romanticism of the 1840s. So too are the roots of de Valera's vision of republican austerity and virtue.

Why, when German Romanticism finally accommodated modernisation, did Irish Romanticism tend, generally, in the opposite direction? A plausible explanation would seem to be that Ireland faced, in an acute form, a common colonial dilemma, whereas Germany did not. Germany's problem was a superfluity of self-government, not an absence, and an absence of representative institutions rather than an incapacity to make them respond sufficiently to popular pressure. Mid-nineteenth-century Germany represented a major European culture in search of a political identity; mid-nineteenth-century Ireland, a subject political entity in search of cultural homogeneity and distinction. For Germans, the interconnection of the drives towards modernisation and unification had long been close, had been specified very clearly in Prussia a generation earlier by the Steinites, and had become even tighter after 1834. In the Ireland of the 1840s, as in several colonial and formerly colonial situations in the present century, a contrary tendency was discernible. Davis and Young Ireland responded to the impulse to reject as alien not merely the established state, but also in a sense the established society. The condition of Ireland under the Act of Union rendered this impulse particularly powerful, in much the same measure as it rendered the obstacles to its realisation particularly formidable. The transport revolution of 1824–45, and the rapid extension of a common language, a common market, a common labour supply and common political and social aspirations seemed, to the Romantics, to be eating away at both separatism and self-identity in Ireland. The omnibus word for all these early nineteenth-century trends and developments is 'modernisation'. Hence, I suggest, the unnoticed but sharp and far-reaching divergence of the German and Irish movements in this matter. What was implicit and groping in Ireland in the 1840s was overt, purposive and systematic in the 1890s. Yet another wave of anti-modernism broke, after the next recoil, in the decade 1916–25. Although this form of populism (using the term in its nineteenth-century Russian rather than American sense) was clumsily grafted, later, on to both the Toneite and the O'Connellite traditions, it had derived from a rival *Weltanschauung*. The cosmopolitanism, universalism and individualism almost unthinkingly presupposed by the late enlightenment men were anathema to all Romantics.

The third major Continental influence to which I wish to draw attention is the somewhat amorphous force which some historians call neo-Jacobinism – the force represented by, say, a man like Blanqui in the France of the Second Republic, of the Second Empire and of the months immediately before the Commune. Here – though this is a more tentative suggestion than in the case of Davis's sojourn in Germany – the critical single event may have been the residence of James Stephens, the father of Fenianism, in the fevered Paris of 1848–52. Neo-Jacobinism proclaimed the absolute morality of popular right. Rousseau-like, it distinguished sharply between the popular will and the will of the majority, or even of the masses. Robespierre-like, it saw the designated party or movement as the vehicle of the popular – or, as it might be in Ireland, the national – destiny. Marx-like, it believed society to be in an actual state of war, and sought to behave accordingly. Its aim was the seizure of the state by force. Thereafter, there would follow what Blanqui described, euphemistically perhaps, as an indefinite period of democratic enlightenment: this was to last until the people could be brought to understand the true nature of the popular will. Later decades were, of course, to add strange mutations, nihilism and anarchism, and the exclusive totalitarian party.

It goes without saying that neither the IRB nor the IRA can be explained simply and exclusively in such abstract or Francocentric terms. In particular, the Irish revolutionary movements had nothing to say about – do not appear to have considered seriously at all – what form of political system (its name apart) would follow a successful revolt. Nor did they respond to the later Continental mutations. None the less, an understanding of the ideological soil from which it sprang is vital to an unravelling of the modern Irish republican mind; and part of this soil is neo-Jacobinism. Neo-Jacobinism may help us to understand the programme of action or the *modus operandi* of Irish republicanism; but what it really illuminates brightly is the revolutionaries' concepts of authority and legitimacy. The Fenians and their successors were not concerned that they were a handful, numerically. In their own eyes, they were the prophetic minority and the trustees for an historic destiny. On them had been laid a heavy and inescapable commission, far above the yea or nay of any evanescent and probably supine electorate. Did not the noblest Roman of them all, much later, express the republican mind most pithily in two famous observations: that the majority had no right to do wrong, and that he had only to look into his own heart to discern the wishes of the Irish people?

I have set down what seem to me to be the three primary or original layers of extraneous ideology which helped to form the Irish nationalist mind. They were laid down (geomorphologically, so to speak) while the plasticity and facile confusion that go with political powerlessness and irresponsibility were still at work. They had hardened before the Protestant *furor Britannicus* had spent itself in the late nineteenth century; before it was apparent that ascendancy in Ireland had changed – had to change – its social, economic and geographic bases; and well before the urge to extra-mural domination and 'imperial necessity' had ceased to be imperatives for most English people.

But from Fenianism onwards, the Continental influences upon Irish political concepts appear to have been comparatively slight. It is true that there have been many and various correspondences between developments in native and foreign ideology or political technique since the 1860s. These, however, would seem best explained in terms of analogy or of expressions of the *Zeitgeist* rather than in terms of causation. Irish dynamards abounded in the decade of dynamards. The explosive became for a time a symbol for the Irish-American left:

> Not a cent for blatherskite
> And every dollar for dynamite.

But how could one go farther – whether arguing the derivative or the originating case – than to say (somewhat unhappily) that dynamite was in the air? Similarly, the foundation of the Gaelic League was more or less contemporaneous with Pobeydonostsev's Russification programme, and there were more resemblances between the two than might seem apparent on the surface – the concept of language identifying the national essence, for example, or the assertion of moral superiority on behalf of the indigenous and customary, or the verbal wall against alien influence which a non-international tongue might furnish. But it seems quite as doubtful that Pobeydonostsev had ever heard of Hyde or O'Growney as that they had ever dreamt of Russian parallels. Again, men like Synge and Yeats, on the one hand, and Pearse and MacDonagh on the other, trod some of the same path as the Narodniks in their respective 'goings to the people'. But who would argue that there was imitation? Yet again, it is notorious that the rise of the forces of anti-parliamentarianism in Ireland in and after 1912 was part of a Europe-wide revulsion from the pacific resolution of conflicts and constitutional forms of politics. More pertinently still, this rise was immediately preceded in both Great Britain and France by the spread of militancy and brutal repression alike in labour, socialist and women's causes – to say nothing of the rash of

> Pale Ebenezer thought it wrong to fight,
> But Roaring Bill who killed him thought it right

doctrines. But the Ulster Volunteers and their southern imitators were looking backwards, not eastwards. They were repeating, in twentieth-century form, traditional Irish patterns. Even Connolly's and Larkin's movement, though initially a development of the contemporary British struggle, soon lost its international air, and became the familiar Irish duel in a packing case. The Citizen Army owed nothing in conception or style to foreign precedents.

It is also true that Arthur Griffith appealed specifically to Friedrich List and the Hungarian precedent in arguing, respectively, for Irish economic self-sufficiency and for a dual monarchy for two essentially autonomous states. But these were props, not sources, for his arguments. They were, so to say, foreign stamps stuck upon Irish envelopes. Protectionism was a necessary ingredient of any case for economic self-sufficiency; and dual monarchy was a very likely refuge in 1905 if one rejected both violence and Westminster, and also sought to square southern separatism with northern 'loyalty'. When we enter, in the inter-war years, a phase in which conscious imitation of Continental ideology was attempted, it is the general failure to fit Irish circumstances, or to take root in the Irish cities, which strikes the observer immediately. Fascism and Bolshevism have been touched on earlier; Corporativism – on the surface, a more hopeful importation – remained in every sense an academic exercise. It beat in vain against a small-proprietorial social structure; a British form of parliamentary system; deep-rooted and fissiparated trade unions; and of course the 'unfinished business' of the Republic.

At first sight, the latest of the ideological incursions appears to belong to the earlier category. The Ulster civil rights movement of the late 1960s clearly derived from the North American, and to a lesser extent continental European, examples, not to mention from a phenomenon common to all the Western world, the rapid expansion of higher education at the mid-century. This tended (to use the language of the day) to detribalise and disclass large numbers of the young, and land them up, uncomprehending and impatient, before the historic networks of social division and discrimination.

But the ultimate moral here is surely, not that Northern Ireland contributed its troop (with the usual roughriders) to an international crusade, but that that troop was swiftly and almost wholly overborne by the ancient passions. Has not, alas, the civil rights movement in the Ulster of the 1960s proved much the same as Corporativism in the Irish Free State of the 1930s: an exotic, flowering for the hour, before it folded and failed in an inhospitable soil?

The general truth then would seem to be that the habits of mind and action which characterise modern Irish nationalism were beaten into shape by foreign influences in the century *c.* 1770 to *c.* 1870. The succeeding century has lived, as it were, in the moulds in which mature Fenianism finally cooled and set. Thus, for example, the medley of fresh concepts and practices thrown up in Paris in 1871 and in the course of the later struggle of the left against the Third Republic appear to have won no response in Ireland; and this is but a single instance of a general ideological frigidity. Reasons for the contraction, however far they may be from a total explanation, are not hard to find. Three suggest themselves immediately.

First, European political theory in the second half of the nineteenth century was deeply affected by the decline in religious belief; the failure of faith in the generation coming to maturity during 1850–70 was particularly marked. In some branches, the effect was one of substitution. The various Continental religions of humanity or of the social organism received even English counterparts. T. H. Green's idealism of the 1880s, for example, was a late reaction to the 'death of God' which replaced the quest for personal salvation by an other-regarding imperative of secular and communal regeneration. In other branches, heartened by the prodigious achievements and claims of the natural sciences, traditional anti-clericalism and materialism were restated and revivified, after their early nineteenth-century retreat. None of this had much relevance to Ireland where the counter-reformation and its counter-spirits were burning, if anything, more brightly. On the contrary, the earlier Irish movements which had started out self-consciously as non-sectarian or extra-religious, or been coloured by anti-clericalism, became by insensible degrees, like O'Connell's parties, distinctly Catholic in tone. Fenianism was fairly baptised during the amnesty campaign of 1869; Pearse's new Fenianism positively conflated the seminarist gallantry of Trent with violent nationalism; and even linguistic and cultural separatism acquired in time a Catholic identification. 'While our peasants say their beads,' observed the *Lyceum* as early as 1890,

> and meditate on the mysteries of the Rosary, they can never come wholly under the sway of the doctrine that men were sent into the

world to be happy and to make money. .... He [Davis] saw in the factory system a monster that destroyed this ideal life, and he was its foe. He would have Ireland a nation of peasant owners.[3]

Secondly, post-1848 European radicalism was increasingly permeated by the idea of social revolution. It is of course a common-place that Ireland was in the toils of a social revolution in the late nineteenth and early twentieth centuries. But this was revolution in a severely limited sense and sphere. It aimed at nothing more than a change in the actual ownership of land, with certain obvious economic and political corollaries. To European radicals, social revolution meant some total reordering (probably by violent means) of the entire body of social relationships. But in Ireland it meant little more than driving out or buying out the landlords. Concepts springing from the European ground could gain no purchase in the Irish countryside. The steady increase in the number of the pro-pertied there, and the steady draining off, by emigration, of the landless class and of so many of the un- or under-employed or insecure, ensured the perpetuation of this immunity.

Thirdly, Ireland lacked the tradition of 'the unfinished revolution'. This is relevant because, paradoxically, such a tradition tends to produce new political fermentations. It may be a matter of massive and many-sided analysis, such as the great Continental upheavals received; or else that the attempt to improve upon 'the dress rehearsal' and carry to completion the 'inchoate' or 'arrested' revolution usually led to significant changes in emphasis – and, ultimately, presuppositions. The great exemplar of this phenomenon was, of course, France, where the struggle to realise '1789' in the 1790s, in 1830, in 1848 and in 1871 led to repeated ideological innovation. But '1789' took the boards as well in Germany and Russia, inspiring the 'dress rehearsals' of 1848 and 1905 respectively, so necessary, doubtless, for the eventual plays of 1918 and 1917; '1789' had, however, nothing to offer Ireland because (to repeat it yet again) the Irish were in an essentially colonial situation. Nor could the native sequence of 1798, 1803, 1848 or 1867 provide models to improve on, or present themselves as stages of a development. Not merely did each seem to posterity, if considered as a precedent for action, dispiriting or irrelevant or both; it was also in the nature of the colonial situation that the conflict should appear as static, not progressive. Popular language sometimes catches nuances which are otherwise missed. It may be of some significance that the entire series from 1798 to 1916 is generally spoken of as 'risings' or 'insurrections' or 'rebellions', not as 'revolutions'; it may even be significant that, in the title of the IRB, 'Revolutionary' soon made way for

'Republican'. In risings, one overthrew the dominating power, or failed. Each attempt was regarded, not as facilitating the next or redefining the object of the assault, but as a sacrifice. It represented the witness borne by the generation concerned to the right to self-determination. Thus, when the ideological limit of simple and absolute republicanism was reached, say, by the 1860s, there was no longer a dynamic element within its system of ideas or view of history. Revolutionary theory is never still, but insurrectionary theory soon congeals. There is, so to speak, no secondary or tertiary fermentation; and the repeated casting of fresh foreign yeasts into the tun over more than sixty years has had no apparent effect beyond that, perhaps, of demonstrating the incompatibility of the two.

IV

The relative immobility of the critical elements in Irish history which we have just discussed may make the task of finding the reflections of present situations in the past less dubious and difficult than usual. Of course, this is always a dangerous exercise: facts may be pressed too hard to make the fit neater; the idiosyncracy of the past moment may drop out of sight; the propensity to predict, to play the prophet, grows. Whatever the dangers, it is worth attempting; in fact, it is always being attempted, whether consciously or unconsciously, by historians. For after all, what is history but a dialogue between present apprehensions and knowledge of what has gone before? To historians, present and past are a pair of burning glasses. Angled rightly, they light up patterns or motifs in one another which suddenly sharpen our perception of both series of events. The extent and the limit alike of what the historian can achieve in this undertaking seem to me well conveyed in de Tocqueville's 'prediction' of the Paris revolution of 22 February 1848. On 29 January he had told the Chamber of Deputies:

Can you say to-day that you are certain of tomorrow? Do you know what may happen in France a year hence, or even a month or a day hence? You do not know; but what you must know is that the tempest is looming on the horizon, that it is coming towards us.

Reflecting on this three years later, he observed:

And now that I am face to face with myself, searching in my memory to discover whether I was actually so much alarmed as I seemed, the answer is no. . . . No, I did not expect such a revolution as we were destined to have; and who could have expected it? I did, I believe, perceive more clearly than the others the general causes which were making for the event. . . .[4]

This indicates exactly the historian's possible advantage. In relating past and present, he may gradually discern 'the general causes', the fundamental correspondences, which (though modified continually by chance and changes in the surrounding circumstances) give a deeper understanding of the sequences and relative position of events.

The best historical illumination of Britain's conduct in Ireland over the past decade seems to the present writer to lie in the age of 'Grattan's parliament'. It is in some respects the illumination of opposites, of mirror images. This is not surprising, for in very broad terms the years of 'Grattan's parliament' represent the stage of fearful aggrandisement by Great Britain, and the present, one of disengagement. Political union is the great common factor, but with Britain intent, then on using the grappling irons, now on casting off.

From 1780 onwards, the view that Anglo-Irish relations were narrowing to a crisis gained ground in the British governing circles. The prophecy, first made in the 1760s, that if Ireland kept to her current course, either separation from or union with Great Britain would soon be an inescapable choice, was being made more often. Men commonly put two decades or even less as the limit in time to the maintenance of the existing system of 'indirect rule'. Why this sense of the nearing rapids and an impending climax? First, because of the apparently irresistible onflow of religious toleration. British political control of Ireland in the eighteenth century rested upon religious discrimination. It was their dependence upon British power for their engrossment of property and privilege which made the British connection seem indispensable to the bulk of Irish Protestants. It did not matter if the Protestants were recent converts from Catholicism – as they increasingly were: this merely created a broader base for privilege, in much the same way as the Reform Act of 1832 was meant to do. It did matter if they were Presbyterians, because, in terms of privilege, Presbyterians faced both ways; it was a very serious question in which direction they would move, whenever a decision was forced upon them. At any rate, the weakening of Protestant, and in particular Anglican, ascendancy seemed an inevitable historical process to the enlightened of the 1780s; and this threw the traditional methods of British domination in Ireland into uncertainty.

Secondly, political reform appeared to be close at hand. The spirit of the age may not have breathed out the idea of fundamental change

F

in Britain, but it certainly did suggest that a more rational, uniform and comprehensive basis for the parliamentary system could not be staved off for long. But after 1782 British power in Ireland depended, mechanically speaking, upon parliamentary abuses and anomalies. In fact, as the course of events in the 1790s showed, it depended upon the steady extension of such malpractices. There was no other means of ensuring Irish parliamentary majorities, and without sure majorities there was no guarantee that British policies, even in essentials, would prevail. Moreover, the American precedent and the general European phenomenon of burgher and aristocratic revolt in the 1780s suggested that trustee or vicarious government was tottering everywhere. In Ireland, it seemed, no more than a modest measure of parliamentary reform was needed to win effective self-determination for a body which was at once colonial, privileged and rich.

It was in these circumstances that the British government used its power in Ireland to force through relaxations of the anti-Catholic penal code. The motivation was doubtless mixed: in part, altruistic and humane; in part, to create an indigenous counterpoise to the Protestant monopoly in Ireland; and in part, to neutralise the potentially dangerous force of resurgent Catholicism there. Who can say what the relative weight of these three factors may have been, in the minds of Pitt and his associates? The point of no return in this checkmating process was reached in 1793 when the British cabinet insisted upon the enfranchisement of the Irish Catholic forty-shilling freeholders. War had both accentuated the importance of control of Ireland, and placed the papacy in the same camp as Britain, equal enemies of revolutionary France. At the same time, the move helped to counteract the pressure for parliamentary reform. It rendered less certain the maintenance of the Protestant ascendancy – at any rate, in the long run – should the political ties between Britain and Ireland ever loosen.

Though with various checks and retreats, British policy proceeded in the same direction until 1795, with the contrapuntal theme of Catholic and other reforms requiring an obdurate stand on, and even increase in, political abuses. Then, when the new coalition government seemed on the brink (however it jibbed and shivered) of compelling the Irish parliament to pass a measure of Catholic emancipation substantially like that of 1829, Pitt at the very last drew back. When the final calculations had to be made – and they could not be made coolly in the crisis precipitated by Fitzwilliam – the risks appeared too great.

It was not that emancipation would have threatened any immediate danger to the status quo. At most, it would have involved the entry of two or three dozen of the Catholic gentry, probably more servile than their Protestant brethren, to the Irish parliament. But it was impossible for any British statesman of foresight in the mid-1790s to suppose that indirect rule through parliamentary corruption could be maintained indefinitely. This being so, emancipation would open a door which could not be closed at convenience (who could have guessed that the disfranchisement of the forty-shilling freeholders would prove politically practicable a generation later or that, by then, 'Catholic' politics could proceed independently in Ireland, no longer needing this electoral battering-ram?). Gratitude – even the humble Catholic gratitude which Pitt heard so much about – was a thing of the hour in politics, but possession of the franchise was another matter. Parliamentary reform, to say nothing of other possible developments, might well give the Catholics a measure of independent power. This might of course be held *in terrorem* over the Irish Protestants. But it might also be held *in terrorem* over Britain's interests in her dependency. Moreover, elements in Irish Protestantism might later, in resentment at their abandonment or to secure some extra-sectarian objects, make common cause with the enfranchised Catholics. Again, there was the British dimension to be considered. Anti-popery was again a rising force in England. In this respect, George III was as much a harbinger of the near future as an anachronistic bigot. As if his personal intransigence were not enough, it was probably the case that he already reflected British opinion in this field more accurately than did his cabinet.

Finally, the Irish executive, dominated by Fitzgibbon, was fiercely opposed to the concession. This was important because the aid of the executive, and in particular that of Fitzgibbon, was indispensable if ever an Act of Union were to be carried in Dublin. Moreover, Fitzgibbon's bold and cynical analysis of the Irish power struggle seemed all too convincing to busy, hard-headed politicians who knew Ireland only from the outside and were therefore susceptible to simplicity. Fitzgibbon insisted that the Irish Protestant community was a beleaguered garrison which had seized, and held, its privileges by force. British arms sustained them in Ireland; nothing else could. They sustained British authority in Ireland; nothing else could. Beneath all the fine sentiments, fair words and temporary conjunctions of the day, this was the stark and eternal reality; and the choice facing the British government was either to maintain the Irish Protestant ascendancy in power, place and property (which sooner or later implied a political union) or else lose the island.

Thus 1795 marked the turning point in British policy; at least, the strategic end of that policy, political control, was henceforward sought by other means. Immediately, the moves towards parity for

Catholics were halted. Later in the year, the failure to use governmental power to shield them from Orange aggression in Armagh, Down and Tyrone, and to amend the Insurrection Bill so as to deal equally with Defender and Orange disturbances, capped Fitzwilliam's recall. All these precipitated the cycle of violence and repression, of Presbyterian and Catholic conflict, of Presbyterian and Anglican *rapport*, and of the change in the mass support of the United Irish movement, which ended in the outbreak of 1798. This did not mean that the British government had determined in 1795 *permanently* to throw its weight behind total Protestant ascendancy, Catholic abasement and a pocket parliament. None of these seemed durable in the long run. A union which converted a large Catholic majority in Ireland into a minority of 20 per cent at most in an amalgamated kingdom, and did away with the necessity for a scandalous and precarious parliamentary order in Dublin, seemed more than ever attractive; 1798 clinched the argument. A Protestant front had now clearly emerged, with security for Protestant lives, interests and property as its over-riding object. At the same time, it would be as dangerous (from Britain's standpoint) to endorse blindly and for the indefinite future the actions of this fear-crazed minority as to crush every hope of further amelioration in Catholic breasts. So the die was cast. Union, coupled with emancipation and suprafactional government, was determined on. But union, when it came, was coupled with other things, the maintenance of the old ascendancy and the retention of the Irish executive, unrepentant. Political ineptitude and cowardice, and unexhausted bigotry, succeeded at the very end in turning Britain's Irish tactics inside out.

Scholarship, artistry and sense alike forbid any attempt to explain, in a simple or literal fashion, recent British policy in Ireland in terms of late eighteenth-century history. Yet it is impossible, I think, to reflect upon the two phases without some feeling of *déja vu* sweeping over one repeatedly. Again and again, so to speak, snatches of the second melody recall the first. To change the metaphor, the strong lines of the early pattern seem to show through the later. Does not the post-1763 mood of Britain, with its new consciousness of empire, remind one of the opposite mood setting in at the Suez disaster of 1956, with empire dead? And is not the first the ultimate context for the drive towards political union, as the surest of controls, and the second for an opposite state of mind in which separation could be contemplated calmly, even wistfully? Again, does not the British participation in a cosmopolitan wave of religious indifferentism and toleration in the 1780s match, more or less, the 1960s? Again, cannot an equal readiness to put off intractable political problems by forcing a course of social and economic parity upon a reluctant Irish executive and parliament be discerned in both phases? Does not 1795 represent essentially the same type of policy reversal as that of mid-1971? Does not the Act of Union bear a true resemblance to the suspension of Stormont – with, in each case, the clear end of one era being accompanied by ambiguity as to the meaning of what had been done or what was to follow?

The temptation to continue long with such a catalogue, or to fill in the interstices, must be resisted. Nothing is easier, or more historically debauching, than to manufacture historical analogues from disparate sets of materials; and the oftener one particularises, the more likely one is to err. Yet, in general terms, the student of Britain's modern policy in Ireland must, I think, find the earlier phase hauntingly familiar. Nor should this seem surprising, or be turned from as a siren call luring to academic shipwreck. The elements, the variables, the issues in question, may have changed their forms and relationships, but none has disappeared. What we have here (as so often in the history of Anglo-Irish conflict) is a special case of an ancient condition. Now it is a case in which the Protestant communities constitute a majority; in which traditional parliamentary reform is powerless to effect a relevant change; in which Britain eschews but cannot avoid ultimate control nor yet return to a latter-day system of 'undertakers'; in which the existence of a Dublin regime has introduced innumerable fresh complications. But in one light all these are but temporal accidents. In terms of the great matters, allegiances, identities, fears, colliding interests, the 1970s are simply the 1790s writ anew. To turn 'Grattan's Ireland' over and over in our minds cannot, I think, fail to deepen our understanding of what de Tocqueville sees as the historian's special vision, 'the general causes' of affairs. Perhaps this understanding may even be the north's last best hope. 'History', wrote Lecky once,

> is never more valuable than when it enables us, standing as on a height, to look beyond the smoke and turmoil of our petty quarrels, and to detect in the slow developments of the past the great permanent forces that are steadily bearing nations onwards to improvement or decay.

Improvement or decay? Once the great permanent forces have been discerned, perhaps some little field of choice has been created.

Notes and References

CHAPTER 2

1 W. L. Burn, 'Free trade in land: an aspect of the Irish Question', *Transactions of the Royal Historical Society*, 4th series, vol. XXXI, p. 68.
2 E. Stokes, *The English Utilitarians and India* (Oxford, 1959), p. vii.
3 R. D. Collison Black, *Economic Thought and the Irish Question, 1817–70* (Cambridge, 1960), p. 243.

CHAPTER 3

1 *Hansard*, 3rd series, vol. CXCVI, 1062 (31 May 1869).

CHAPTER 4

1 R. D. Collison Black, 'William James Pirrie', in C. Cruise O'Brien (ed.), *The Shaping of Modern Ireland* (London, 1960), pp. 182–3.
2 T. M. Healy, *Letters and Leaders of My Day*, vol. II (London, 1928), p. 562.

CHAPTER 5

1 T. P. Coogan, *Ireland Since the Rising* (London, 1966), p. 70.

CHAPTER 7

1 I am indebted to M. Wall, 'The Whiteboys', in T. D. Williams (ed.), *Secret Societies in Ireland* (Dublin, 1973), pp. 13–25, for the account of this eighteenth-century agrarian movement. In describing the Whiteboys I have drawn upon my contribution to *Perspectives in American History: Volume X, 1976,* ed. D. Fleming and B. Bailyn (Harvard University Press, 1976).
2 I am indebted to J. S. Kelly, 'The political, intellectual and social background to the Irish Literary Revival to 1901' (unpublished PhD dissertation, University of Cambridge, 1972), for the quotations used here and other material on Davis.
3 *Lyceum* (August 1890), quoted in P. O'Farrell, *Ireland's English Question* (London, 1971), p. 229.
4 A. de Tocqueville, *Recollections* (ed. J. P. Mayer) (London, 1948), pp. 14, 16.

Further Reading

The great bulk of scholarly writing in recent Irish history dates from 1939, in which year *Irish Historical Studies* was first published. Because the field is so newly (and as yet far from completely) worked, some of the important material is contained in learned journals, and not yet in books; accordingly, several articles are included in the list of suggested readings.

A few books to which the present author is particularly indebted for material not to be found elsewhere are marked below by an asterisk.

GENERAL

Much the best general histories covering most of our period are J. C. Beckett's excellent survey, *The Making of Modern Ireland: 1603–1923* (London, 1966) and F. S. L. Lyons's *Ireland Since the Famine* (London, 1971), though an earlier standard work with a longer time-span, E. Curtis's *History of Ireland* (6th edn, London, 1961) is still useful. N. Mansergh, in *Ireland in the Age of Reform and Revolution* (London, 1940), analyses briefly but with great penetration certain aspects of nineteenth-century history; and P. O'Farrell's *Ireland's English Question* (London, 1971), and E. R. Norman's *History of Modern Ireland* (London, 1971) both contain highly stimulating and original viewpoints. T. W. Freeman's *Ireland, its Physical, Historical, Social and Economic Geography* (London, 1950) is a good introduction to the aspects indicated by its title, and two general works of L. M. Cullen, *Life in Ireland* (London, 1968) and *The Formation of the Irish Economy* (Cork, 1969) are warmly to be commended as introductions to social and economic developments. R. D. Crotty's important pioneering study, *Irish Agricultural Production: Its Volume and Structure* (Cork, 1966), has recently been supplemented by those of two American scholars, B. Solow, *The Land Question and the Irish Economy* (Harvard, 1971) and J. S. Donnelly, Jr, *The Land and the People of Nineteenth Century Cork* (London, 1975); and another American scholar, R. E. Kennedy, has opened up other features of recent Irish social and economic history in his *The Irish: Emigration, Marriage and Fertility* (Berkeley, 1973).

P. S. O'Hegarty's *Ireland Under the Union, 1801–1922* (London, 1952) is highly partisan, but lively and informative, and G. Locker Lampson's *A Consideration of the State of Ireland in the Nineteenth Century* (London, 1907), though heavy and eclectic, contains material and viewpoints of great interest not to be found elsewhere. T. P. Coogan's *Ireland Since the*

Rising (London, 1966) is a pioneer work for the years 1921–65, to be recommended for its manner as well as its matter, and several of the essays in *The Course of Irish History*, edited by T. W. Moody and F. X. Martin (Cork, 1967), a collection of broadcast talks by distinguished Irish scholars, are noteworthy. Various attempts have been made to view modern Irish history through the spectacles of economic determinism, but E. Strauss's *British Democracy and Irish Nationalism* (London, 1951) is the only Marxist interpretation of real merit. Irish Unionism has now been extensively reviewed in a work of that title (2 vols, Dublin, 1972–3) by P. Buckland. *Irish Historical Documents 1172–1922* (London, 1943), edited by E. Curtis and R. B. McDowell, includes much original material for the years of the Act of Union. It is the only comprehensive collection of documents in this field.

1800–50

G. Ó Tuathaigh's short survey, *Ireland Before the Famine* (Dublin, 1972), is an excellent introduction to the pre-famine period, and its companion in the series, J. Lee's *The Modernisation of Irish Society, 1848–1918*, is a stimulating essay; and two books by R. B. McDowell, **The Irish Administration 1801–1914* (London, 1964) and *Public Opinion and Government Policy in Ireland: 1801–46* (London, 1952), are very useful. The first deals with the structure of central government in Ireland under the Act of Union, and the second conveys well the climate of opinion and the reactions to British rule in the years before the Great Famine. G. C. Bolton, in *The Passing of the Irish Act of Union* (Oxford, 1966), explains the circumstances and immediate implications of the passage of the statute. The main Irish issue of the early nineteenth century, Catholic emancipation, is dealt with effectively in G. I. T. Machin's *The Catholic Question in English Politics 1820–30* (Oxford, 1964) and J. Reynolds's *The Catholic Emancipation Crisis in Ireland: 1823–29* (New Haven, 1954). *The Liberator* (London, 1956), by A. McIntyre, is not a biography of Daniel O'Connell but an analysis of his political conduct and the management of his political 'party' between 1830 and 1847; there is no large-scale modern biography of O'Connell, but W. E. H. Lecky's *Leaders of Public Opinion in Ireland* (2 vols, new edn, London, 1912) throws considerable light upon his public career.

A. H. Graham, 'The Lichfield House Compact', *Irish Historical Studies*, vol. XII, is a valuable examination of the formation of the Irish-Whig alliance, one of the dominant features of Irish history in the 1830s and 1840s; and R. B. O'Brien's *Thomas Drummond: His Life and Letters* (London, 1889) illuminates the reforms undertaken during Melbourne's administration. K. B. Nowlan's *The Politics of Repeal* (London, 1966) covers the later stages of O'Connell's career and the early history of the Young Ireland movement. *The Great Famine* (Dublin, 1956), edited by R. D. Edwards and T. D. Williams, is a symposium which deals with the social, economic, demographic, political and medical aspects of the disastrous potato blights of the late 1840s and early 1850s; C. Woodham

Smith, *The Great Hunger* (London, 1962), extends this examination in a few areas. The economic history of Ireland in this period (or for that matter in any period) is a comparatively undeveloped subject. G. O'Brien's *The Economic History of Ireland from the Union to the Famine* (London, 1921), although unsatisfactory in several respects, is an indispensable source book.

Special aspects of the subject are covered satisfactorily by K. H. Connell, *The Population of Ireland, 1750–1845* (Oxford, 1950); H. Senior, *Orangeism in Ireland and Britain, 1795–1836* (London, 1966); D. H. Akenson, *The Irish Educational Experiment* (London, 1970); G. Broeker, *Rural Disorder and Police Reform in Ireland 1812–36* (London, 1970); P. Lynch and J. Vaizey, *Guinness's Brewery in the Irish Economy: 1759–1876* (Cambridge, 1960), which also puts forward some general hypotheses; and R. D. C. Black, **Economic Thought and the Irish Question: 1817–1870* (Cambridge, 1960), which analyses admirably contemporary economic theory, its effects upon Irish policy, and the counter-effects of Irish conditions upon the academic speculators. See also an important paper on nineteenth-century Irish demography, S. H. Cousens, 'Emigration and demographic change in Ireland, 1851–1861', *Economic History Review*, 2nd ser., vol. XIV.

1850–1900

The political history of this half-century, especially on its constitutional and parliamentary side, has been examined systematically in a recent succession of monographs of a high calibre: J. H. Whyte, *The Independent Irish Party, 1850–59* (Oxford, 1958); E. R. Norman, *The Catholic Church and Ireland in the Age of Rebellion* (London, 1965); D. Thornley, *Isaac Butt* (London, 1964); C. Cruise O'Brien, *Parnell and His Party, 1880–90* (Oxford, 1957); and F. S. L. Lyons, *The Fall of Parnell* (London, 1964). All of these books are good representatives of modern scholarship, and O'Brien's is something more, 'a classic'. They are supplemented by a number of important papers which illuminate particular episodes or facets of the subject: P. J. Corish, 'Cardinal Cullen and the National Association of Ireland', *Reportorium Novum*, vol. III; J. F. Glazer, 'Parnell's fall and the non-conformist conscience', *Irish Historical Studies*, vol. XII; D. C. Savage, 'The origins of the Ulster Unionist Party, 1885–86', *Irish Historical Studies*, vol. XII; and T. W. Moody, 'Parnell and the Galway Election of 1886', *Irish Historical Studies*, vol. IX.

A number of contemporary Irish politicians either began their careers as journalists or combined journalism and politics, and though none of their books is dispassionate, several contain information, critiques or interpretations of great value. The most interesting are perhaps C. G. Duffy's *Four Years of Irish History, 1845–49* (London, 1883) and *The League of North and South* (London, 1886); William O'Brien's trilogy, *Recollections* (London, 1905), *Evening Memories* (Dublin, 1920) and *An Olive Branch in Ireland* (London, 1910); T. M. Healy's *Letters and Leaders of My Day* (2 vols, London, 1928); and T. P. O'Connor's *The Parnell Movement* (London, 1886). The period is poor in biographical material, but R. B. O'Brien's *Life of Charles Stewart Parnell* (2 vols, London, 1899) and T. de Vere White's life of Isaac Butt, *The Road of Excess* (Dublin, 1946) are valuable.

J. L. Hammond's *Gladstone and the Irish Nation* (London, 1938) remains the best work on mid-Victorian Liberal policy toward Ireland, but the Conservative counterpart is now better covered in an admirable study by L. P. Curtis, Jr, *Coercion and Conciliation in Ireland, 1880–92; A Study in Conservative Unionism* (Princeton, 1963). There is no modern work of major significance on Fenianism but J. O'Leary's *Recollections of Fenians and Fenianism* (London, 1929) and W. O'Brien and D. Ryan (eds), *Devoy's Postbag* (2 vols, Dublin, 1948, 1953) contain valuable matter, as does the collection of essays edited by T. W. Moody under the title, *The Fenian Movement* (Cork, 1968). The agrarian question in the closing decades of the nineteenth century is dealt with in J. E. Pomfret, *The Struggle for the Land in Ireland* (Princeton, 1930). See also M. Davitt, *The Fall of Feudalism in Ireland* (London, 1904).

THE TWENTIETH CENTURY

Four collections of broadcast talks by Irish and British historians, **The Shaping of Modern Ireland* (London, 1960), edited by C. Cruise O'Brien; *The Irish Struggle* (London, 1966), edited by T. D. Williams, *The Years of the Great Test, 1926–39*, edited by F. MacManus (Cork, 1967), and *Ireland in the War Years and After, 1939–51*, edited by K. B. Nowlan and T. D. Williams (Dublin, 1969), provide valuable introductions to the leading movements, events and personalities of the late nineteenth and early twentieth centuries. In several instances, there is no other source which can be recommended. A good general survey of the years 1910–21 is contained in E. Holt, *Protest Under Arms* (London, 1960); for a similar survey for the period after 1921, see Mr Coogan's book, listed above.

There is no single book on the closing stages of the struggle for Home Rule, but several tell various parts of the story. The most important of these are F. S. L. Lyons, *The Irish Parliamentary Party* (London, 1951); two books by D. Gwynn, *Life of John Redmond* (London, 1932) and *The History of Partition* (Dublin, 1950); H. M. Hyde, *Carson* (London, 1953), R. B. McDowell, *The Irish Convention, 1917–18* (London, 1970); F. S. L. Lyons, *John Dillon* (London, 1968); and two analyses of the Curragh 'mutiny', by A. P. Ryan (London, 1956) and Sir J. Fergusson (London, 1964) respectively. The standard biographies of almost all the leading British politicians of the years 1900–18 also contain some useful material on this question; of particular interest is R. Blake's biography of Bonar Law, *The Unknown Prime Minister* (London, 1955). Something of the history of a constitutional 'rival' to Home Rule – the Co-operative movement – can be found in H. Plunkett, *Ireland in the New Century* (London, 1904) and M. Digby, *Horace Plunkett, an Anglo-American Irishman* (Oxford, 1949).

Sinn Fein has as yet received comparatively little attention, but R. M. Henry's *The Evolution of Sinn Fein* (Dublin, 1920) and P. Colum's *Arthur*

Griffith (Dublin, 1959) are useful. Initial work of first importance on the Easter Rising has been done by F. X. Martin in his collections of documents, with commentaries, *The Irish Volunteers: Recollections and Documents, 1913–15* (Dublin, 1963), *The Howth Gun-Running* (Dublin, 1964) and 'Eoin MacNeill on the 1916 Rising', *Irish Historical Studies*, vol. XII. The details of the 1916 fighting in Dublin are recounted in M. Caulfield, *The Easter Rebellion* (London, 1964); and these collections, *1916: The Easter Rising*, edited by O. Dudley Edwards and F. Pyle (London, 1968), *Leaders and Men of the Rising*, edited by F. X. Martin (Dublin, 1967) and *The Making of 1916*, edited by K. B. Nowlan (Dublin, 1969), illuminate many aspects of the movements which led up to 1916, and of their culmination.

Republican and Unionist versions of the independence struggle as a whole are provided in two partisan but nonetheless very important books: D. MacArdle, *The Irish Republic* (4th edn, Dublin, 1951) and W. A. Phillips, *The Revolution in Ireland* (2nd edn, London, 1926). R. Bennett's *The Black and Tans* (London, 1959) attempts to rescue the force under discussion from total obloquy. The best survey of the Civil War to date is that of C. Younger (London, 1968). Two major works which contain most illuminating comments on the Irish troubles and their conclusions are W. S. Churchill's *The World Crisis: The Aftermath* (London, 1929) and W. K. Hancock's *Survey of British Commonwealth Affairs: Problems of Nationality 1918–36* (Oxford, 1937). F. Pakenham's *Peace by Ordeal* (London, 1935) provides an excellent analysis of the treaty negotiations of 1921; see also F. Gallagher, *The Anglo-Irish Treaty* (London, 1965). Perhaps the best biographies of Irish leaders in the War of Independence are those of Collins by R. Taylor (London, 1958), M. Forester (London, 1971) and P. Beaslai (2 vols, Dublin, 1926); S. O'Faolain's *De Valera* (London, 1949); *Eamon de Valera* (London, 1970), by Lord Longford and T. P. O'Neill; and T. de Vere White's *Kevin O'Higgins* (London, 1958).

Good special studies on the Irish Free State (and its constitutional successors) include J. L. McCracken, *Representative Government in Ireland* (Oxford, 1958); D. Harkness, *The Restless Dominion: The Irish Free State and the British Commonwealth of Nations, 1921–31* (London, 1968); L. Kohn, *The Constitution of the Irish Free State* (London, 1932); B. A. Chubb, *Source Book of Irish Government* (Dublin, 1964); and D. O'Mahony, *The Irish Economy* (Cork, 1962) and J. Meenan, *The Irish Economy since 1922* (Liverpool, 1970). For Northern Ireland, up to 1968, see N. Mansergh, *The Government of Northern Ireland* (London, 1936); *Ulster Under Home Rule* (Oxford, 1955), edited by T. Wilson; and K. S. Isles and N. Cuthbert, *An Economic Survey of Northern Ireland* (Belfast, 1957).

Index